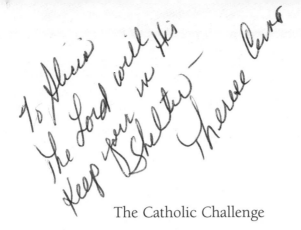

The Catholic Challenge

The Catholic Challenge
Six Keys to a Deeper Spiritual Life

THERESE CIRNER

SERVANT
BOOKS

PUBLISHED BY ST. ANTHONY MESSENGER PRESS
CINCINNATI, OHIO

Library of Congress Cataloging-in-Publication Data

Cirner, Therese.
  The Catholic challenge : six keys to a deeper spiritual life / by Therese Cirner.
     p. cm.
  ISBN 1-56955-291-6 (alk. paper)
  1. Spiritual life—Catholic Church. I. Title.
BX2350.3.C57 2004
248.4'82—dc22
                              2004011817

Cover design by Steve Eames
Book design by Mark Sullivan

ISBN 1-56955-291-6
Copyright ©2004, Therese Cirner
All rights reserved.

Published by Servant Books, an imprint of St. Anthony Messenger Press.
www.AmericanCatholic.org
Printed in the U.S.A.

04 05 06 07 08 5 4 3 2 1

To Randall, my husband,
with profound thanks for everything.

Contents

INTRODUCTION

I came that they may have life, and have it abundantly.

—JOHN 10:10

Stephen Covey, a successful business and family man, wrote the best-selling book *The Seven Habits of Highly Effective People*. In it, he observes that men and women who have reached some level of success have certain characteristics in common.

Covey notes, for example, that people who are successful start with the end in mind: they have a clear vision of their goal before they set out to achieve it. Accordingly, he suggests that people articulate where they want to end up in life then plan their lives in a way that will allow them to achieve that goal. Covey uses a clever device to help his readers focus: he encourages them to spend a few minutes writing their own obituary. Yes. Your own obituary! What would you like to see written about you when your life is over? Then live every day toward achieving that end.

Say, for example, that one of your goals is to own a home by the time you retire. What practical steps should you take toward that goal? One plan might look something like this:

- Research the geographical area where you'd like to live. Talk to realtors and local banks.

- Begin to look at properties within your price range.

- Go to a banker or to a web site that calculates mortgage rates and figure out what your monthly payment would need to be to pay off the house before the age at which you hope to retire.

Now let's apply Covey's thought-provoking technique to our spiritual lives. Personally, I would like to have my obituary read: "Therese Cirner lived her life in a way that was pleasing to God. She was welcomed into the kingdom of heaven with joy." This is a laudable goal but general and vague. Exactly what would I need to do today to move toward that happy outcome?

If you were to search Scripture you would find that Jesus emphasizes six spiritual habits as necessary for all Christians. These habits are the foundation for growth and perseverance in the Christian life. They are: prayer, reading Scripture and books related to the spiritual life, receiving the sacraments, living the communal dimension of our faith, growing in virtue, and extending forgiveness. These habits will help us grow and will sustain us in times of temptation, trial, boredom and fatigue. Jesus gives an incredibly clear map for success in his best-selling book, the Bible. He didn't leave cryptic clues or vague directions on how to get to heaven.

"Why do you call me 'Lord, Lord' and not do what I say?" he asks his listeners as he tells the parable about the house built on rock and the house built on sand. The person who "comes to me, hears my words, and acts on them," he says, is like the person who digs deep and lays his foundation on rock (Lk 6:46-49).

Jesus said that we must not only hear his words but act on them or put them into practice. *Practice* means "to do or perform repeatedly so as to master" or "to cause to perfect by repetition." The *American Heritage Dictionary* offers a definition with elements pertinent to the Christian life: to drill, exercise, brush up, rehearse, train, repeat. When we apply these elements to the habits identified by Jesus—when we drill, train, repeat and so forth—the habits will become almost automatic. This discipline is important. Some days we will feel in the mood to pray or read Scripture, while other days we may not be in the mood to do anything other than what pleases us at the moment. But if we have trained ourselves in self-discipline, godly habits will help carry us through.

Setting Out on the Journey

All this talk of discipline and habits, however, should never obscure the fact that our time on earth is an adventurous journey—exciting, daring and fulfilling. Like every journey, it is filled with peril and intrigue, joy and pain but this particular adventure—your life—ends with a prize: the crown of eternal life. And this adventure has a common theme for all of humanity: each of us longs for love with every fiber of our being. That love is named Jesus, love is a person.

How do we come to know that love? This book is for the "everyday" Catholic who has wondered what to do next in the spiritual life. If you've ever asked yourself such questions as: "How can I grow closer to God?" "Am I so boring that I'm putting God to sleep?" or "How do I 'hear' God?" then this is the book for you.

For a variety of reasons, most Christians don't have a spiritual director or a regular confessor to help them sort through fundamental questions about Christian living. Also, books on spiritual direction as well as many spiritual classics may be daunting to the everyday reader. This book, with its focus on the six keys to holiness, is intended to launch you gently into the essentials of Catholic life with all the depths and richness of our heritage.

In the early years of my own journey, I had only vague ideas about what to expect in my relationship with God. Dare I expect anything? What can an everyday person like me hope for? I had read classic spiritual writers like Sts. John of the Cross, Francis de Sales, and Teresa of Avila but found it difficult to translate John's poetry into a here-and-now understanding or maneuver my way around the many "rooms" in Teresa's *Interior Castle*. My primary goal in writing this book is to offer spiritual adventurers like myself a bridge between our personal journeys and the wisdom of the great spiritual masters. Our spiritual fathers and mothers can, indeed, reach through the years and teach us.

This book is meant to remind Christians that, as the great masters tell us, there is more, so much more. That *more* is a deep, intensely personal love relationship with our God, one that is not based on emotions or feelings but is simply a sharing in the love of the Trinity in this life. We don't have to wait for heaven. This great news is not often advertised!

We humbly accept that reason or knowledge alone cannot bring us to complete understanding. However, a combination of reason and faith can enable us to enter this mystery, for indeed it is a mystery.

I recommend that you keep your Bible handy as you read this book. You will benefit more from the numerous Scripture quotations and references if you can read them in context. You will also want a pen and perhaps a journal. The chapters are arranged to encourage real spiritual growth and include workbook-style questions, meditations and reflections that encourage the reader to respond in writing. *The Catholic Challenge* is intended for individual use as well as for use in small parish groups or similar informal gatherings. It is appropriate for all ages from teens on up—any adventurer hungry for more of God.

FIRST THINGS FIRST

*I am the Alpha and the Omega, the beginning and the end.
To the thirsty I will give water as a gift from the spring
of the water of life.*

—Revelation 21:6

One thing in life is sure: Jesus has set his heart on you. Not only does he want you to be with him in heaven enjoying the love of the Trinity, Jesus is offering that shared love here and now. He died on the cross to save you and he is still loving and saving you today. He never quits.

There is never a time in the Christian life when we outgrow the simple truth of God's love for us. Some of us, however, aren't so sure about that love or we've never experienced it. Before we explore the six keys to effective Christian living, we need to consider what it means to surrender to God and what we might expect from a relationship with him.

It's not unusual for Catholics to have low expectations when it comes to encountering the living God. You may have said things like this: "Priests and religious, the pope—they experience

God. I'm just an ordinary, everyday Catholic." "It sounds too emotional; I don't trust it. I'm content without any personal experience of God." "To be Catholic means to go to church on Sunday, send my kids to religious education, give money to the church and try to be good. I can handle that."

But whether we are saints or sinners, Jesus offers each of us a personal relationship with him. This amazing fact requires a response: we can choose to say "Yes, my Lord and my God"— or we can say no and walk away. Whatever our choice, his choice is to love us and reveal himself to us. These encounters with God comes in as many shapes and sizes as there are people because his love for each of us is custom designed.

Four Ways to Encounter God

The Lord always meets us where we are, usually in one of the following ways:

- Through the natural maturity of childhood faith
- Through a conversion experience after a crisis of faith
- Through an intellectual conversion
- Through a combination of the above

Marianne's Story. Marianne's life with God is an example of childhood faith that grew as she matured. The grace of the sacraments stimulated the seed of faith; this developed in a relatively uninterrupted manner into a mature relationship with God. People like Marianne instinctively love God and have faith in him: troubles come their way but they keep their attention fixed on the cross.

Mari, as she is known, grew up in a large Catholic family in a California suburb. As a child, she was confident that Jesus was with her and she could turn to him for anything. Even as a teenager and young adult, she never doubted God's presence. When she was a student at a large state university, she was upset when professors mocked churches whose beliefs weren't politically correct. In order to understand their perspective, she decided to spend one day acting as if she had no faith. She couldn't keep up the pretense for even ten minutes.

Mari did examine her faith and embrace it as an adult but her spiritual journey does not include some of the twists and turns and doubts that others might experience. Crises of faith were not hers to bear. Mari's awakening was a flowering of the grace of baptism, unfolding as she matured.

Joe's Story. Sometimes people encounter God so dramatically that their lives are never the same. They have been changed in the core of their being and can name the exact day and time when they invited Jesus into their lives.

Joe's dad had a violent temper and drank heavily. Joe tried to stay out of his way and swore that he would never drink nor would he treat anyone the way his dad had treated him. As an adult, however, Joe found himself stopping every night at the local bar after his shift in the factory. Married and with a growing family, he relied on alcohol to relax after a hard day. As the years rolled by he became violent and verbally abusive, just as his dad had been. But Joe knew that something had to change when he did the unthinkable and hit his wife.

Denny, a coworker, noticed Joe's pain and hopelessness. Denny had experienced a life-changing encounter with Jesus after years of struggling with similar issues. He began to sit with Joe during lunch and prayed for him daily, asking the Lord to give him an opportunity to share the good news of salvation.

One day the opportunity presented itself and Denny told him his story. Tears streamed down Joe's face as he recognized his need for a Savior. "There's nothing I can lose. My wife and kids avoid me. I can't stand to look at myself in the mirror. My life is a mess. Am I too late? Can God love someone like me?"

Joe understood, as only the lost do, what it means to be found by a Savior. He surrendered his life to Jesus and prayed: "Lord, I know that I've screwed up big time but if there is any way that you can salvage my life, I promise that I will be one of your disciples. Forgive me. Don't abandon me!" At that moment Joe knew in every cell of his body that God had saved him and that this God loved him.

Joe soon realized that he needed to repent to his wife and children. One Sunday afternoon he gathered the family in the living room and as he looked around, he saw pained and angry faces looking back. He drew a deep breath and began to share about his journey since meeting Denny. When he finished, he knelt before his wife and asked her forgiveness for the years of neglect and abuse. He took a basin of water and washed her feet, imitating Jesus at the Last Supper. Then he knelt before each one of his children and washed their feet, confessing his sin to them. He assured each one that they did not have to immediately forgive him; they should take as much time as they needed. He would understand.

Joe is now past retirement age and is the patriarch of three generations. Since that Sunday afternoon years ago he has genuinely tried to communicate the Father's love to each of his children and grandchildren. When he fails, he asks forgiveness and he doesn't let a day go by without telling his wife he loves and cherishes her.

Joe's story illustrates the dramatic change that can occur when a person welcomes Jesus into his heart. The sure sign that this change was more than an emotional experience is that twenty years later this man is spending his retirement loving and serving God in any way he can. Joe has a special ministry for lost sheep like himself.

Janice and Richard's Story. God also breaks into lives through intellectual enlightenment. People who respond to this approach sometimes feel that life is futile and engage in endless dialogue with others to sort through questions such as: "What does it mean to live a good life?" "How can one know if there is an afterlife?" "How can one know that there is an order in this apparent chaos?" The Lord is a persistent lover who will lead those who genuinely seek truth to the books and the people who will guide them home.

Janice and Richard, college sweethearts, met in Bible college in the Midwest. Both were studying to be pastors, Janice specializing in worship and evangelism, Richard in Scripture. For his senior thesis, Richard chose to write about the breaking of bread at the Last Supper. As he studied each Protestant denomination's theology of the Last Supper, he began to explore Catholic theology of the Eucharist. Initially, he took energetic delight in exposing what he regarded as the blatant error of transubstantiation: The body and blood of Jesus! Really!

Some of the scriptural footnotes in the Catholic *Catechism* intrigued Richard and he began to research them. He was intellectually and spiritually honest and wanted to fairly represent Catholic understanding of the Last Supper. Richard discussed his struggle with his wife and with his academic advisor, both of whom encouraged him to expose the error of the Catholic Church. In spite of this encouragement, his enthusiasm to condemn Catholic "heresy" waned while his personal curiosity increased.

The Holy Spirit used this academic pursuit to bring Richard and ultimately, Janice, into the Catholic Church. For those who pursue an intellectually honest path, the Holy Spirit is there to inspire, guide and teach the minds of skeptics, agnostics and atheists.

My Story. My own story combines the seeds of childhood faith converging with the merciful grace of salvation in an encounter with God. This resulted in an intellectual and whole-life conversion.

A sweet childhood love of God preceded my encounter with Jesus as an adult. I was the fourth of six children. Mom had suffered complications from several miscarriages in the years preceding my birth and prayed for intercession to St. Thérèse, the

Little Flower, for a safe pregnancy and delivery. Since my last name was Martin, my parents named me after her—Therese Martin. I kept her picture on a shelf in my room and when I returned after school, I was sure that she smiled a loving hello to me. I shared her love for Jesus: some nights I would squish onto the furthest edge of the bed to make room for the baby Jesus in case he needed a place to sleep that night. I prayed and knew my prayers were answered.

Ultimately, adolescence was not a time of spiritual growth for me. Drawn into the culture of the 1960s, I chose rebellion, cynicism, depression, and a decided drift away from faith toward agnosticism. I stopped going to church and immersed myself in a search for truth: Ayn Rand's rugged individualism, the existential angst of Camus and Sartre, and the dark Russian soul of Dostoyevsky. During my high school years, I also picketed stores that sold pornography and demonstrated for the civil rights of minorities and against the Vietnam War. I devoted myself to somehow trying to get life right for others and myself. Meanwhile, my brother Ralph—who had experienced a radical conversion to God—was praying for me, as were the Sisters of Charity who taught me in high school. They didn't give up. I went to college, hoping that a more sophisticated environment would help life make sense to me.

Freshman year: Surrounded by interesting people, I was studying what I wanted at a college in a gorgeous New England coastal town. As with most eighteen-year-olds, I was glad to be away from home and held high expectations for my new freedom. Initially, I was fascinated by the intellectual insights of some of my philosophy and existential psychology professors. By the end of the semester, however, I found the academic material less satisfying. Parties, dates, plays, and stimulating conversation filled the hours between classes. Yet I was restless, pensive, never satisfied. I considered changing my major or transferring to a college I had heard about in Vermont. I never suspected that the root of my rest-lessness was a hunger for God.

Dissatisfied with campus life, I explored radical politics as a solution to human suffering. A loosely connected group of students from various East Coast colleges and universities met to explore solutions to the problem of unequal distribution of wealth. We concluded that the answer lay in a new social and political order; working within the system was like using a band-aid to fight cancer. We agreed that when we met in the fall, after summer break, we would begin in earnest.

My brother invited me to spend that summer in Ann Arbor, Michigan, where he worked as a lay campus minister. I accepted, hoping that a new environment would dull my depression and internal pain. Ralph arranged a job for me and set me up with two roommates who turned out to be irritatingly cheerful and loving. Didn't these Christians realize what the real world was all about? If they did, they certainly wouldn't be saying things like, "God will take care of it" and "Praise the Lord." They would be more cynical and empty, like me.

Setting the Spiritual Scene. Serious seekers of truth flourished during the mid- to late sixties but so did immorality, bringing with it the evil of abortion. Drug abuse and sexual promiscuity under the guise of free love proliferated in adolescent and young adult culture. But grace abounds during times of social unrest and our God delights in pouring out his Holy Spirit during periods of moral bankruptcy. One way he did that was to infuse the Catholic Church with a fresh outpouring of the Holy Spirit, just as in the early church. Amazingly, Catholics were filled with the Holy Spirit in an unexpected way. Faith became a burning flame within them, giving these Christians an unquenchable desire to spread the good news of the gospel to anyone who would listen.

That was the situation I walked into when I arrived in Ann Arbor in June, 1968. These Spirit-filled Christians frequently gathered to pray and seek God, sometimes meeting informally in each other's houses or apartments. But they also met more formally every Thursday evening in the basement of the Newman Center of the Catholic student parish.

I went to a Thursday night prayer meeting to satisfy the insistent invitations of my brother's friends. I tried to figure out the psychological dynamics that produced such a profound effect in participants. Surely the indirect lighting created an atmosphere of relaxation; the music swayed the emotions. Internally, though, I felt challenged. I had taken pride in the fact that I would pursue truth regardless of where it led, but I had dismissed religion as the path to truth. What if all these people were right? What if God were the path to the truth that I sought? That would be disappointing, I concluded. The more romantic, visionary side of me preferred the ideas of my friends who spent all night discussing how to right the financial and political injustices in the world. In comparison, this God thing seemed too tame, or so I thought.

In keeping with my promise to pursue truth wherever it led, I sat in the last row of the prayer meeting, closed my eyes and considered an honest and fair response to the possibility that a Supreme Being was the object of my quest. The words from Scripture began to form in my mind: "Love the Lord your God with all your heart, and with all your soul, and with all your mind" (Mt 22:37).

Internally, I worked through the logic. *If* there is a God and *if* he is who they say he is, then the only worthy response is full allegiance to him. At that moment, a light began to spread throughout my being and I felt an indescribable joy. Tears ran down my face. *Jesus*—my Savior, my Lord! I knew the risen Lord and I knew that he would not *lead* me to the truth, he *was* the truth.

Thank God, I was never the same. That summer I pondered how to integrate my living faith and sense of the abiding presence of God with my concern for injustice. I realized that my college friends and I were right about one thing: the current political, economic and social systems could never cure the world's problems. The only authentic remedy for injustice and inequality is the coming of a radical new world order, the kingdom of God. Only a Savior—Jesus—could save this planet.

Your Story. Are you restless? Feeling dissatisfied with your life? Do your relationships lack something? After you've achieved a goal you've worked hard for, do you still find something missing in your life? If you've answered yes to any one of these questions, you could have a case of "longing for heaven."

We are designed by our Creator to find this earthly life less than satisfying. We yearn for true intimacy, true love, and true freedom. However, no man, no woman, no child, no accomplishment, no amount of money, no reverent prayer can ever replace the bliss that the soul knows is possible. Our souls were created for heaven and for real, satisfying intimacy with the Trinity. Nothing less than union with God will bring that profound sense of joy and peace.

The first step on our spiritual journey home to heaven and to true happiness is to understand the basic cause of our longing. Changing the details in our lives could be like rearranging the deck chairs on the *Titanic*: regardless of how the chairs are arranged, the ship will still sink! A new academic major or a new house or new clothes or more money or a new spouse may just mask the real source of restlessness—longing for heaven.

Conversion: Staying the Course. Conversion stories are deeply rooted in Scripture. Remember Paul's encounter with Jesus on the road to Damascus (Acts 9:1-9)? When people encounter God in a personal way, lives change. Scripture is bursting with the Good News of salvation in very real lives. Mary Magdalene, possessed by demons, encountered Jesus and changed dramatically (Lk 8:2). Paul, who hunted down and persecuted Christians, encountered the light of God and changed forever.

But what happens to all those who hear the gospel, refuse to say yes to the Lord Jesus, and walk away from him? Or what about those who initially say yes and then over the weeks, months or years that follow, allow their yes to become a "sometimes," a "maybe" or a "later"?

Jesus addressed various responses to his invitation in the parable of the sower (Mt 13:1-9, 18-23), a story that focuses on a farmer scattering seeds on the ground. Birds eat some of the seeds; some seeds thrive for a time and then wither; weeds choke other seeds; and some fall on good soil and yield a great harvest. A parable is a story that illustrates a spiritual truth, and in this case, Jesus is describing the manner in which people receive the word of God.

The Seed on the Path: Hard-Heartedness. Jesus says, "When anyone hears the word of the kingdom and does not understand it, the evil one comes and snatches away what is sown in the heart; this is what was sown on the path" (v. 19). The path Jesus refers to here is the hardened soil of a fallow Israeli field. Travelers often took shortcuts across such fields, eventually turning the shortcut into a hardened path. The seed represents the truth of the gospel and the hardened ground represents the heart of the one who hears that truth but refuses to accept it. Unable to put down roots, the seed lies there until the evil one swoops down and snatches it.

Jessie, for example, attended a men's retreat one winter and heard the Good News of salvation. Inspired, he decided to be more serious about his spiritual life. As spring began to thaw the frozen ground, however, Jessie sat through Sunday sermons mentally improving his golf swing. On one occasion, the priest described his own spiritual journey and then invited everyone in the church to ask Jesus more deeply into his or her life. Jessie was momentarily stirred to renew his commitment. "I wonder if this is what I need to get back on track…?" Then he glanced at his watch, remembered his upcoming golf match, and began to visualize the first tee at the country club.

Jesus warns us of the work of Satan who is at war, literally, against the kingdom of God. Jessie heard about the love of Jesus but the evil one "swooped down" by way of nothing more than a distracting thought, snatching the seed that lay on the hard ground of Jessie's heart.

The Seed on Rocky Ground. Jesus also talks about seed landing on rocky ground: unable to take root, it is scorched by the sun and withers. So it is with a person who receives the Good News with joy but falls away when trial and persecution arise.

Kathy had recently moved to Minneapolis from a smaller town three hundred miles west of the city. She landed a new job in public relations, joined a church near her apartment, and started attending a Monday evening course on the catechism.

Kathy soon learned that her values clashed with those of her coworkers who were caught up in a superficial lifestyle. The public relations department met at a local restaurant after work every Monday for "happy hour" and Kathy, wanting to fit in, joined them. As the others learned of her personal convictions regarding premarital sex and the sanctity of life, they mocked her and dismissed her views as naïve and old-fashioned.

Kathy put the Monday course at the church aside while she developed her career and tried to make a good impression. Soon she no longer remembered why she had originally been so uncomfortable with these men and women. They were urbane, intelligent, and they began to accept her. She was flattered.

Kathy started out on the right track, received the seed of the gospel with joy, and joined a church and a study group. But she gave up this necessary means of support and spiritual growth in order to grow professionally. The heat of flattery and a non-Christian environment scorched the seed of faith. Sometimes "trouble or persecution…on account of the Word" is disguised in ways we may not anticipate, such as pride, a need to achieve, and fear of social embarrassment.

The Seed Among Thorns. "As for what was sown among thorns," Jesus continued, describing yet another circumstance in the parable of the sower, "this is the one who hears the word, but the cares of the world and the lure of wealth choke the word, and it yields nothing" (v. 22).

Elizabeth and Mark were teenagers in the late 1970s. They met at a summer youth conference on teen evangelization, gave themselves wholeheartedly to Christ, and then began to work with other teens in evangelization. They married after college. Elizabeth taught grade school while Mark went to graduate school and worked part-time in his dad's business. They prayed together and served together, ministering to teens through their parish youth group.

Eventually they had three children and as the pace of family life increased, they began to sink under the weight of financial, emotional and physical stress. Mark's business was successful and required more time on the road. The children had hectic schedules. As the years passed, it became difficult to get the kids out of bed for church on Sunday mornings. Elizabeth and Mark convinced themselves that they needed a day of rest more than they needed a "formal" church service on Sunday.

We can all relate to the stresses of modern life and this family's life sounds all too familiar! But the thorns that Jesus speaks of are not life's many demands themselves: rather, it is allowing those demands to choke off the source of life. We can't slide into heaven on the momentum of past spiritual growth. Yes, the road of discipleship is hard and rocky but the effort required to walk that road is eternally worth it.

The Seed on Good Soil. Finally, Jesus speaks of the person who not only hears but also understands the call of God. "As for what was sown on good soil, this is the one who hears the word and understands it, who indeed bears fruit and yields, in one case a hundredfold, in another sixty, and in another thirty" (v. 23). This individual internalizes and acts with devotion and purpose to bring about the reign of God. His response is deep, wholehearted, and unending.

Sonja and Steve worked together in youth ministry and their lives evolved in a pattern: children, financial struggles, physical illnesses, and relationship strains. But they never stopped placing the Lord at the center of their individual lives and their life as a couple and family. God was the central motivating force for all they did and all they were. They both were sensitive to the Holy Spirit prompting them to share the good news of the saving love of God with anyone, whether it was in the grocery store or at work. They enjoyed vacations and good books and the ordinary things of life but the Living Water was always at the center of their lives.

The result of staying faithful and true to the gospel is the promised yield of one hundred, sixty or thirtyfold. Sonja and Steve were faithful to their commitment to Christ and persevered in their ministry despite the temptation to rationalize that fervor is for the young, that they couldn't keep this up forever, that they deserved some time off. This spiritual abundance will be experienced in their own lives, their children's lives, and all whom they have served.

The most exciting and challenging adventure for each of us is this journey that begins with the awakening and ends with the prize, the crown of eternal life. As we faithfully maneuver this earthly life with its love and healing, perils and temptations we will find ourselves drawn into union with the Trinity. Impossible? Not at all. When we surrender to God and pursue the habits that strengthen us in our spiritual walk, all things are possible.

For Reflection
Think back on your life. Were there people who passed on the faith to you? Who prayed for you, talked to you about the Lord, and laid the foundation for your faith? Have you thanked these people for their faithfulness?

Can you recall times when the Lord seemed close to you, extending an invitation to say yes to him? How did you respond? What happened as a result?

Prayer

Jesus, I know that you are the Lord, my savior, my redeemer, my friend. I long to drink deeply from the waters of eternal life. In your mercy and love, please change my heart of stone into a heart of flesh like yours. Make me into your image. Fill me with your Holy Spirit.

Continue this prayer with your own words.

THE FIRST KEY

PRAYER

Pray without ceasing.

—1 THESSALONIANS 5:17

Prayer is as essential to us as breathing, eating and sleeping. Connected to the source of life, we receive the grace to persevere and resist sin. And just as in human relationships, when we spend time with God we cultivate our friendship with him, get to know him, understand him more and confide our needs and dreams to him. And consider this: God really, personally loves us. He knows all the little and big things in our lives, what makes us laugh and what makes us cry, how we long to be loved by another, how our heart breaks when one of our family or friends is not in the state of grace.

This intimate relationship with God based on his saving love is unique to Christianity. Intimacy with God is available to all, although each of us will experience that intimacy according to our own personality, degree of surrender to the Lord, and God's own knowledge of and plans for us.

In prayer we find strength, joy, the means to express our grief or pain, repentance, worship, praise and longing for God. Without prayer, we will not advance in the Christian life. With it, we have the key that opens the door to all the treasures of heaven.

Spontaneous words directed to God seem natural. These words are the beginning of prayer. For me, my first prayer as an adult was, "If you exist, Lord, if you are who they say you are, then I give you my life."

After that first foray into verbal prayer, I discovered a wide range of prayer that I hadn't known existed. I grew up in a Catholic family, attended Mass on Sundays and holy days. My family prayed the rosary together—especially during Advent and the month of May—and said grace before meals. My dad went on weekend retreats every few years and I found my mom reading *The Imitation of Christ* by Thomas à Kempis during the few quiet moments she enjoyed. As a child, I knelt at my bedside and found words to beg Jesus for that red dump truck and doctor's kit I wanted so desperately one Christmas. Yet I knew little of prayer beyond this.

Recollection

All thoughtful prayer should begin with recollection. Words will prove empty and fall to the ground unless we understand that our Lord wants more than our words, he wants our hearts. The purpose of prayer is to draw us into union with the living God. Recollection prepares us for this union; it is the time when we collect our thoughts and energy from other interests, duties and people, put them aside, and enter the presence of God. Recollection has three elements.

What are we doing? When we come to prayer, we are opening the lines of communication with the Trinity: Father, Son and Holy Spirit. We offer our love, awe, and reverence as well as our emptiness and sinfulness, our hopes and petitions. In turn, we learn to listen intently to the movement of the Holy Spirit within us.

Why are we praying? It is not only right to pray and give God the glory, praise and worship due him. Prayer also fulfills the desire of our heart to know God, to draw close to him, to share our deepest concerns with him who loves us. We also pray because prayer opens us to receive the grace, love and healing he longs to give us.

Who is listening? Our God is the creator of the universe, the Lord of Lords and King of Kings, our lover, our friend, the Lamb that was slain, the Savior of the world and our personal Savior. He is all in all. We are in awe of his mighty love and humble before him yet amazingly, we rest our head on his knee as he comforts us. God is both the Supreme Being and the most intimate companion, all in one. If we have an "I want, please give me" shopping list approach to prayer, we will need to put away our list at the beginning of our prayer time to focus on who God is and to give him our love and affection.

These three W's— what, why, and who—are the first stages of any prayer. Our minds and bodies, preoccupied with the normal minutiae of life, need this time of recollection so that we can orient ourselves to the things of God.

Once we have established ourselves in these first stages of prayer, we need to cultivate a spirit of determination if we are to progress. Determination is essential to success in any area and the spiritual life is no exception. St. Paul made this clear when he described his own approach to life:

> I have fought the good fight, I have finished the race, I have kept the faith. From now on there is reserved for me the crown of righteousness, which the Lord, the righteous judge, will give me on that day, and not only to me, but also to all who have longed for his appearing.
> —2 Timothy 4:7-8

We would do well to apply to our prayer life the same sort of perseverance and determination shown by two well-known people, a modern fast food genius—Colonel Sanders—and a French saint, Thérèse of Lisieux, the Little Flower.

Colonel Sanders of Kentucky Fried Chicken fame spent years experimenting with, testing and developing his recipe for fried chicken. He had a restaurant on a heavily traveled road but a new superhighway thirty miles away diverted traffic from his restaurant and it soon failed. Sanders believed in his product, however, and so, at the age of sixty-two, he went from restaurant to restaurant offering owners his recipe for a percentage of their profit. Time after time, they turned him down.

If you had that recipe, how many times would you have accepted rejection before giving up and going home? Fifty times? One hundred times? Five hundred? Colonel Sanders was rejected nearly a thousand times before someone bought his recipe for fried chicken. He believed in his product, he was determined and we know the rest of the story!

St. Thérèse brought the same dogged persistence to her efforts to enter the convent. In her autobiography *The Story of a Soul*, she relates that she was convinced that she had a vocation to be a cloistered Carmelite nun, just as two of her sisters were. The major obstacle was that she was only fourteen years old at the time.

She waited but when she was fifteen the superiors at Carmel refused her early entrance into the Carmelite order. Her parish priest and her bishop refused her request as well. Undeterred, Thérèse, on a pilgrimage to Rome with her father, boldly prevailed upon Pope Leo XIII himself to grant her an exception. With a group of pilgrims, she attended an audience with the pope. Priests warned the crowd that they were absolutely forbidden to speak to Pope Leo but Thérèse ignored the rules. When her turn came to approach him, she later wrote, she found herself "at the Holy Father's feet. I kissed his slipper and he presented his hand, but instead of kissing it I joined my own and lifted tear-filled eyes to his face, I cried out: 'Most Holy Father, I have a great favor to ask you.'"

The Holy Father not only refused her request but also directed her to return to her local superiors saying, "Go...Go...You will enter if God wills it!" Little Thérèse remained where she was. "As this was not enough they took me by the arms...for I stayed there with joined hands resting on the knees of Leo XIII." Two guards lifted her up and literally carried her out of the room.

When we, like Thérèse, humbly receive the love of Jesus into our hearts, allow desire for him to blossom, and add determination to the mix, we have a winning combination. In Thérèse's case, she entered Carmel the following year.

Our personal stories may never be known as St. Thérèse's is known, but much hinges on our desire for God, determination to achieve our goal, and persistence in prayer.

Types of Prayer
Formal Prayer The church has a broad collection of formal prayers including everything from the Our Father to the prayers of the early church fathers to prayers of contemporary saints. These prayers, in varying moods and styles, articulate the heart of humanity's intimate relationship with God.

I remember clearly the time a close friend of mine died; I was so numb that I couldn't talk to God in my own words. I was relieved that I had a prayer book so I could come before the Lord but with someone else's finely crafted words.

And sometimes, formal prayers allow us to minister to others when we aren't up to it. My daughter Jennifer was recovering from brain surgery and was heavily sedated. She had begun to have small seizures that we later learned were a reaction to a drug. Here was my adult daughter in such pain that I could barely concentrate to pray for her. I had a prayer book with me at the hospital and looked for something to console her and keep her focused on the Lord. When she regained consciousness, I began to quietly read some of the prayers for healing. After the first two prayers, she began to move her hands together. "Jen, what's wrong?" She answered, "Mom, I was trying to clap my hands. That was a good one."

One pitfall of formalized prayer is that repetition in and of itself does not necessarily deliver quality. Repetition can just dull the senses allowing the mind to wander while the voice repeats words. St. Teresa of Avila wrote pointedly to her sisters that moving the lips and forming words to be heard by others cannot pass for real prayer. However, St. Francis of Assisi once spent the whole night praying one Our Father. As we stressed earlier, recollection is the key to successful formal prayer.

Informal Prayer. Informal prayer is that which we offer in our own words. Early in my walk with Jesus, an older Christian told me about a format called ACTS that provided some structure and balance for my informal personal prayer:

A: Adoration. Begin by giving the Lord the praise and worship due him: *You alone are worthy, Lord. Jesus, you are the holy One of God. You are my Redeemer and my Savior.*

C: Contrition. Acknowledge your generally sinful nature and mention specific sins. Include any mortal sins (of course, these need to be confessed to a priest as soon as possible), deliberate venial sins, and any personal failings that have offended God or others. Spiritual maturity will bring with it an added awareness of omission, failure to do good: *Father, I come before you so aware of my unworthiness, of my sin that is an offense to you who are so good, so loving. In your mercy, forgive me my sins and offenses.*

T: Thanksgiving. Thank the Lord for his unfailing love in your life, his faithfulness to you, his forgiveness, and his protection: *Thank you Jesus for your love and your mercy, which is never ending. Thank you for caring for me the way you do and sending your angels to watch out over me and my family. I rejoice in you.*

S: Supplication. This is the time to present your needs to God, your loving Father. This can include everything from prayer for family members who have strayed from the faith, to financial problems, to a simple request that he give more of himself to you. Don't hesitate to ask—persistently. Jesus himself strongly encourages us to ask that our needs to be met. Remember the Little Flower—the Lord delights in answering the determined Christian. Read Luke 18:1-8. Jesus uses the story of a very persistent widow as an example of how to pray correctly.

Informal prayer also includes just speaking to Jesus when we think of it, whether we're driving to work or cooking dinner. As we get up in the morning, we might ask him for the grace to get through the day: "Jesus, you've got to help me keep my temper today. It's more than I can handle. Just be there with me and give me the grace. Please, form me into your image, the only one I desire." Also, sometimes during repetitive tasks such as walking or folding laundry I pray informally for intentions people have brought to my attention.

Praying in the Holy Spirit. Many Catholics find this means of prayer effective and powerful. Sometimes words seem inadequate, especially at painful or profound moments. Speaking in tongues or praying in the Holy Spirit is a gift of the Holy Spirit that should not be overlooked. And who better to help us pray than God himself in the person of the Holy Spirit?

When I realized that the Holy Spirit was a real and present help for me, and when I invited him into my life, I couldn't wait to tell my friends. I called Alex, a friend from high school, and he surprised me by asking me if he could have the Holy Spirit too. I thought about it for a moment and told him I saw no reason why not. Since I had asked for the fullness of the Spirit at a prayer meeting, we arranged that he would be at his church in New Jersey the next Thursday evening during my next prayer meeting in Michigan. The pastor allowed him to use the church for an hour and Alex and I agreed that he would ask for the Holy Spirit at the same time that I would ask the people in Michigan to pray for him to receive the Spirit.

The Lord is good. As we carried out our plan, Alex was filled with the Holy Spirit and began to pray in a new way. I understood then that anyone can ask for the infilling of the Spirit regardless of whether anyone else is present. But there is evidence in Scripture for the "laying on of hands" (for example, see Acts 8:17; 9:17) There is power when Christians gather to pray, sometimes actually laying their hands on the person they are praying for.

Was it my idea to think of Alex and give him a call? Perhaps. More likely it was the inspiration of the Holy Spirit. This inspiration does not come accompanied by trumpets and angels, at least not in my experience. The Holy Spirit more often gently nudges me to get my attention.

But how do we know that an apparent inspiration is from the Holy Spirit? It could be a good idea or just a random thought or impulse. Cultivating a life of prayer is essential to hearing the Spirit, but discernment and experience are the key ingredients that help us know it is him we hear.

For starters, we should understand that the Holy Spirit will never lead us to do anything wrong, hurtful or stupid. This is the first level of discernment. If the matter is important, we should discuss it with a more experienced Christian who can offer additional discernment.

Sometimes we'll have to step out of our comfort zone. When I thought to call Alex, I hesitated and wondered what he might think of all this God talk. But I knew I was offering him the best of everything.

Examine the fruit of a suspected prompting of the Holy Spirit. Look at the results of being led by the Spirit. My desire to call Alex has borne lasting fruit. He is still a lay leader in his Catholic community and is raising his four children in the faith.

A friend, Joanne, told me an inspiring story of a time she was led by the Spirit. Joanne was in her twenties and a student at a public university, enduring a class with a professor who was particularly antagonistic toward her. When the class went on field trips, the professor opened his "rolling bar" and encouraged the students to drink.

Some students complained to the authorities and the professor stood in front of class at the end of the semester in tears, regretting his poor behavior. The disciplinary board was to meet with him during semester break. Joanne went home after taking the final exam and realized that this man whom she despised was perhaps having a change of heart. She felt that the Lord wanted her to send him a letter and enclose a prayer card and a rosary with it. In the letter she encouraged him to look to God for his answers regardless of the outcome of the disciplinary board. She told him that she would be praying for him,

On Christmas Eve, while Joanne and her family were at Mass, this professor called and left a message on her answering machine. He thanked her for the letter and her prayers. He was changing his life and was going back to church for the first time in ten years.

Stories like this indicate the rewards of being more sensitive and obedient to the promptings of the Holy Spirit. I understood, when I received the sacrament of confirmation, that I was entering God's army. This is true. We are all soldiers for the King and his kingdom.

Communal Prayer. "Where two or three are gathered in my name, I am there among them" (Mt 18:20). Jesus promises that he will be present with Christians who come together to pray, either formally at Mass or other church services, or informally. What consolation, what power!

Although some people find it awkward to pray with others, the rewards are immense once you get started. See if there are small prayer groups in your parish. Praying the rosary as a family is a wonderful tradition—as are regular family prayer times or grace before and after meals. Be willing to start small and be led by the Spirit.

Singing. St. Augustine described singing songs to the Lord as "praying twice." Song unites the heart, mind, voice and spirit in worship of the living God in a manner that other forms of prayer do not. Scripture often refers to singing to the Lord; the Book of Psalms is a collection of 150 songs. The Book of Revelation in the New Testament describes heavenly song:

> Then I heard every creature in heaven and on earth and under the earth and in the sea, and all that is in them, singing,
>> "To the one seated on the throne and to the Lamb
>> be blessing and honor and glory and might
>> forever and ever!"
> And the four living creatures said "Amen!" And the elders fell down and worshiped.
>
> —REVELATION 5:13-14

Meditation. St. Teresa of Avila describes meditation as the conversation between the lover—Jesus—and the beloved—you and me. The joy of meditation is that it helps us transition between verbal prayer and nonverbal "being with" the Lord.

Meditation is like a quest. In meditation we use our imagination and emotion to grasp something more about a spiritual truth such as the mercy of God or the life of the Trinity or forgiveness or redemption. It leads us into the "more" that is available to us. Through meditation, we increase our internal capacity to understand and just be with God. There are numerous methods of meditation but remember, a method is a structure to help guide us; it does not and should not constrain the work of the Holy Spirit.

The *Catechism of the Catholic Church* describes *meditation* as follows:

> Meditation engages thought, imagination, emotion, and desire. This mobilization of faculties is necessary in order to deepen our convictions of faith, prompt the conversion of our heart, and strengthen our will to follow Christ. Christian prayer tries above all to meditate on the mysteries of Christ, as in *lectio divina* or the rosary. *This form of prayerful reflection is of great value, but Christian prayer should go further: to the knowledge of the love of the Lord Jesus, to union with him.* (CCC, #2708, emphasis mine)

In meditation we use Scripture, spiritual reading, our imagination or a holy object not only to inform ourselves but also to inspire within a new depth of spiritual understanding. These reflections serve as the springboard for loving conversation with our Lord. As we meditate, our hearts respond in love, faith and hope so that the Holy Spirit can teach us the things that God desires for us.

Projecting yourself into a gospel story can be a useful technique for meditation. For example, the story of Jesus meeting the disciples on the road to Emmaus is one of my favorites. In this post-resurrection account, two disciples meet Jesus but fail to recognize him. Jesus readily takes up the role of teacher: "Beginning with Moses and all the prophets, he interpreted to them the things about himself in all the scriptures" (Lk 24:27).

Open the Gospel of Luke and reread this story (Lk 24:13-35). Imagine yourself as another disciple on the road to Emmaus, walking with the other two. Identify environmental details such as your clothes, the smells, the temperature. Then ask Jesus the questions in the text; ponder your feelings as he walks along with you (v. 15); enter into the sorrow of the puzzled disciples (v. 17); what are your feelings as Jesus breaks the bread? (v. 30); experience the joy of that late night return to Jerusalem to announce your encounter with the Lord (vv. 33-34). Thank him for his revelation of himself to the disciples and to you. Stay in that scene and ask the Holy Spirit to teach you what he wants you to learn through these verses.

In our meditation, Jesus invites us to develop an ever-deeper, more personal relationship with the Trinity through the action of the Holy Spirit. That requires a willingness to venture, in some ways, into the unknown. This, of course, demands desire and determination: desire to have more of God in our lives and determination to persist until we do.

My friend Clint's experience of meditation might help clarify what depths await us in this type of prayer. Clint often went to weekday Mass in a Franciscan chapel close to where he worked. The chapel had stained glass windows that depicted different scenes from the life of St. Francis. One day as Clint prayed, he could not keep his attention from the window that showed Francis embracing a leper. The fingers, nose and toes of the leper were eaten away by the disease and St. Francis had his arms around him, his head resting on the sick man. At the bottom of the window was the traditional figure of Satan, red with tail and horns, hatred distorting his face as he fled the scene.

Clint felt the Lord wanted him to meditate on this window. He asked himself, "Who is the 'leper' that the Lord wants me to embrace?" Clint knew that he should not begin to busily list people or situations that he thought might fit that description; instead, he knew that he should wait for the Lord to show him the answer. This "being with the Lord" in silence is the gateway into meditation and then contemplation. Clint told me that God then drew his attention to Satan in that picture. "The Lord showed me that when I embrace the leper or lepers in my life, Satan will flee." It occurred to me after my conversation with Clint that perhaps Jesus is in the role of St. Francis in my own life and I, in my spiritually diseased condition, am the leper. His love and healing send Satan fleeing.

Contemplation. Contemplation is a wonderful gift from the Trinity. In it, the Holy Spirit quiets our minds and we enter into a deeply silent union with God. This spiritual stillness cannot be confused with sleepiness or dullness. We are acutely aware of and present to the Spirit of God—his love, his awesome holiness, and our unworthiness. Words cannot adequately describe this union.

Individuals who experience the transition into this gift of prayer are usually reluctant to speak of it because it is so intensely personal and holy. Clint, my friend who meditated on the leper and St. Francis, progressed from meditation to contemplation. When I asked him about this, he quietly said that he had struggled for most of his adult life with doubts about whether God truly heard his prayers, whether God loved him as much as he loved others; Clint wondered if he would ever be welcomed into the kingdom of heaven.

Clint's doubts diminished as he entered the world of contemplation and gained the type of assurance that only the Holy Spirit can bring. He realized that something significant had shifted in his spiritual life. He did not have to work at focusing on the Lord in his prayer time: Clint entered into the presence of the Lord as smoothly as if walking from one room into another. He found that throughout the day, when he shifted his attention to the Lord, the connection with God was immediately present. It wasn't that Clint had done anything different, God just gave him this gift of greater spiritual union with him.

When to Pray

Prayer is simply loving, talking and being with God and letting him love us back. In his First Letter to the Thessalonians, Paul tells his readers: "Rejoice always, pray without ceasing, give thanks in all circumstances; for this is the will of God in Christ Jesus for you" (1 Thes 5:16-17). Praying without ceasing implies that Christians can be in God's presence all day, every day: we can silently speak to him as we go about our daily responsibilities of family and work. Brother Lawrence, a seventeenth century monk, made this point in his book, *The Practice of the Presence of God,* which still guides and inspires Christians today.

More specifically, the complement to praying in the spirit "without ceasing" is to establish a more formal time when you stop all other activity and focus on the Lord. I have found that setting a specific length of time to pray, perhaps half an hour, helps me stay long enough to pray and prevents me from popping up and leaving prematurely when I get distracted. On days you are particularly distracted, pray with your Bible in your lap for ready inspiration or a rosary in hand to guide your mind. If a half hour is too long or too short, adjust the time to your walk with the Lord. Start with five minutes—or even one minute—but do it every day. The important thing is not how you pray or how long, but that you stay connected with your Lord and Savior every day in some way.

Sometimes laziness, attachments to other activities, poor planning or poor self-control interfere with prayer. Other factors may come into play, however, such as taking care of children all day and half the night or holding an extremely demanding job.

When God calls us to a vocation—whether as a parent, wage earner or in any other role—he understands the limitations placed on us by that vocation and will provide grace to grow closer to him as we live out that call. When my children were young and I had laundry piled high, I decided that instead of complaining that I had no quiet time for prayer I would intercede for the family member whose clothes I was folding. I listened to praise and worship tapes while I prepared dinner. And I had several small New Testaments hidden strategically in the bathroom, under the cushion of the rocker, and in the car where I could read while I waited for kids to show up from an activity.

Now that my time is a bit more my own, I'm able to go to daily Mass, pray the rosary while I walk, and intercede while doing housework—spiritual multitasking.

A friend of mine commuted by train for a total of three hours every day. He solved the no-time-to-pray problem by doing a Bible study every morning on the way to work and praying the rosary every evening on the return trip. Would he have preferred one hour in a chapel praying and reading Scripture? Sure. But with a little creativity, discipline and openness to God's grace, he made lemonade out of lemons.

Praying in Your Own Way

Of course we can and should grow in our prayer life—that usually happens over time—but we should also realize that heaven rejoices when anyone prays. It pleases God when you come to him in prayer, anytime, anywhere.

One day I was praying in a local chapel when I heard the side door open. Instead of hearing footsteps head toward a pew, I heard them head to a group of statues of the Holy Family located on the side of the chapel. I turned to look. A man who was obviously mentally challenged put his hand on each of the statues of Mary, Joseph, and Jesus.

Breathlessly and with no trace of self-consciousness, he said out loud, "Hi, Mary. Hi, Joseph. Hi, Jesus. Boy, they sure are keeping me running today and I still have a lot of work to do. I hate to make this so short but I wanted to let you know in case I don't make it back. Tell the Father I said hi and explain it to him. Thanks."

As the door closed behind him, I realized that I had overheard an incredibly profound prayer. I know the Father was pleased by this man's simple prayer, a simplicity we can all aspire to.

Imagine God

No human understanding of God is complete. God is far beyond our ability to imagine, and yet we must have an image of him that will inspire us in our prayer life. Knowing Jesus and praying to him is a great foundation for prayer. But Jesus himself tells us that if we know him we will know the Father. When Philip asks Jesus to show them the Father, Jesus replies: "Whoever has seen me has seen the Father. How can you say, 'Show us the Father'? Do you not believe that I am in the Father and the Father is in me?" (Jn 14:8-11).

There can be very human reasons, however, for finding it difficult to pray to the Father. Religious art, for example, while often inspiring, sometimes presents an intimidating view of God the Father. Artists tend to portray him sitting in the heavens with wild uncombed white hair and a hellfire-and-brimstone look on his face. He seems more than a little angry.

Our personal experience of our own fathers can also be an obstacle to a relationship with God the Father. Do a quick internal check and make sure that neither religious art nor negative experiences with men in authority have created a false representation of our Father in Heaven. For those struggling with negative feelings, I recommend the book, *The Return of the Prodigal Son: A Story of Homecoming* by Henri Nouwen, listed in the resource section at the end of this book.

We can enhance our image of Jesus by using the concordance in a study Bible to enrich our appreciation of him. Look up and meditate on different traits he exhibited during his three short years of public ministry: for example, his compassion (Mt 11:28-30; his authority (Lk 8:22-25); his joy (Lk 10:21). It can also be a good investment to purchase religious art that appeals to you and inspires you to love him.

Understandably, the Holy Spirit—often represented as a dove, fire, wind or breath—offers a less concrete image than Jesus or the Father. But when you received baptism and confirmation, you received this third member of the Trinity into your soul. He is already with you and within you. Ask him to reveal himself to you, to love and guide you, and you will find yourself growing in awareness of and reliance on him.

Setting a Place

Since prayer is an encounter with the living God within us, prayer is quite portable! You can pray on your knees in your bedroom or sitting in the living room. I've even captured moments of prayer while sitting in the sun pretending I was trying to get a tan. That's the great news. Sometimes praying at home can be a distraction: "I'll just make one more phone call then I'll pray." In that case, going to a church or adoration chapel helps us focus on the Lord. Crucifixes, statues, kneelers are all conducive to prayer and recollection.

Some Christians create a prayer corner or prayer room in their homes where they have holy pictures, a pillow for kneeling or sitting, and perhaps some candles. Such an arrangement might help you quiet your mind for prayer.

As you cultivate a prayer habit, your special "place" for prayer is likely to be more a matter of your state of mind rather than your physical location. So, if you cannot set aside a regular place for prayer, at least try to have a reverent attitude.

Staying Focused

Frequently, the time we set aside for prayer is the first time we have all day to stop, sit down, and pull ourselves together. All the cares and concerns that have accumulated vie for our attention during that quiet moment. Money, parents, jobs, children, health, legal and financial problems and relationships of every size and sort clamor for our attention. Of course, we want God to know about these things—and fix them. But is this prayer or distraction?

I suggest writing down a list of the worries and cares you want to bring before the Lord. Then recollect yourself before the Lord, perhaps reading a psalm or prayer. As the worries pop up and preoccupy you, tell yourself that you have written down that concern to pray for later and you won't forget. Speaking this truth to yourself is a good way to silence the worry gremlins at prayer.

If they are very persistent, you may want to take your list and intercede more intently in prayer, saying a rosary for all these intentions or praying the Divine Mercy chaplet during the first part of your prayer time. That way you can reassure yourself that yes, you did pray for all your needs and yes, God has heard you.

Remember, if you suffer from distractions in prayer, you are in good company! St. Teresa of Avila and her Carmelite sisters struggled with the same problem. In *The Way of Perfection*, Teresa writes:

> O Sisters, those of you who cannot engage in much discursive reflection with the intellect or keep your mind from distraction, get used to this practice! Get used to it! See, I know that you can do this; for I suffered many years from the trial—and it is a very great one—of not being able to quiet the mind in anything.

She suggests the following remedies.

Don't give up—even if it takes years. Teresa urges us to remember that the intimacy with God gained through prayer is eternally worth the time and effort put into it.

"Look at him," she says. Even if just for a moment, it is beneficial. He is the spouse longing to have his beloved glance at him. We can glance at him with the eyes of our soul or with the eyes in our head. Having holy cards, pictures and crucifixes helps the distracted mind focus even for the moment.

Place yourself with our Lord in a scene of the Gospel. Walk with him, hear him, and let him speak to you.

Bring a contemporary book on the spiritual life to prayer. As distraction strikes, we can read another sentence or paragraph or page, then "glance at God."

Most important, never give up or lose hope. Persevere in prayer and you will grow more in love with God.

In addition, the time of day that you pray might influence the degree to which you are distracted. Sometimes it can help to pray first thing in the morning before all the cares of the day have dug a trench in your thought life. Studies have shown that people who want to develop an exercise habit stick with their program longer if they exercise first thing in the morning. Perhaps a similar regimen will shape up your prayer life.

Staying Interested

What does it mean when you start to find it boring to pray? Sometimes what appears to be boredom is really the Holy Spirit nudging us into a deeper prayer life. Ask the Lord to give you more of himself and to transform your heart into his heart. Don't be shy. The Lord wants to pour himself out on his children. Ask the Holy Spirit to fill you to the fullest and then ask and ask again.

Also, be open to different styles of prayer: if you kneel, try standing up; if you usually fold your hands, try opening them as if receiving a gift; if you usually pray silently, try speaking out loud to him. Sometimes these small changes can create a spiritual opening enabling us to receive more of him whom we love.

Staying Positive

Many people suffer from spiritual low self-esteem. This can happen when a Christian observes others and assumes everyone else has a closer relationship with God than they themselves do. In fact, they might merely be observing superficial differences.

Keep in mind that there are many different personality styles. Some individuals experience life more emotionally than others. "Don't you just feel exhilarated in the fall?" a person might ask. You might express your opinion about the season in a more low-key manner: "I look forward to the fall." Maybe you wouldn't express an opinion at all. But don't assume that what someone else is describing is different from and better than what you experience in a very natural way.

And it is true that the Lord works in different people in different ways. As Paul said to the Corinthians:

> If the whole body were an eye, where would the hearing be? If the whole body were hearing, where would the sense of smell be? But as it is, God arranged the members in the body, each one of them, as he chose. If all

were a single member, where would the body be? As it is, there are many members, yet one body.

—1 CORINTHIANS 12:17-20

Be alert, though, to ways that the Lord may want to move you out of your routine or your comfort zone. Feelings and experiences are secondary to desiring more of God in your life. Feelings come and go, but he is the love that lasts forever.

Unfortunately, guilt and shame are familiar companions to many Christians. Have you gone to the sacrament of reconciliation and confessed these sins and discussed your situation with a priest you can trust? This might sound obvious, but sometimes guilt and shame can keep us from the very sacrament that can heal us.

Look to Scripture to learn how God views forgiveness. Psalm 51, for example, is one of the penitential psalms, full of the certainty of God's loving forgiveness:

> Purge me with hyssop, and I shall be clean;
> wash me and I shall be whiter than snow.
> Let me hear joy and gladness;
> let the bones that you have crushed rejoice.
> Hide your face from my sins
> and blot out all my iniquities.

—PSALM 51:7-9

Remember that God sent Jesus to be the sacrifice for our sins. He saw your sins and died willingly for them. They are covered by his blood. And he himself told us that he came to call "not the righteous but sinners" (Mt 9:13).

When your thoughts begin to drag you down, counter them with praise and truth. When you experience God calling you to a deeper relationship with him, and then find yourself mentally and spiritually assaulted with guilt, speak the truth to that guilt: Jesus died for you, he knows that you are a sinner, he loves you anyway.

Enjoying the Fruit of Prayer

The primary fruit of prayer is that we become more like Jesus. We are characterized by love. In place of our hearts of stone, we receive hearts of flesh. The fruits of the Holy Spirit—love, joy, peace, patience, kindness, goodness, faithfulness, gentleness and self-control—are increasingly evident in our lives.

We do not achieve perfection, but the inclination to love—simply, humbly, and in imitation of Christ—is the hallmark of God's life in us. It can transform our lives and the lives of those we love.

For Reflection

Do you desire the Lord and eternal life with him but lack the determination to pursue your goal? Examine and list any contradictions between desire and the necessary determination in your life. What can you specifically do to eliminate even one contradiction?

List the types of prayer that you have already integrated into your relationship with God. What forms of prayer do you need to develop and utilize more often? Why?

The three "W's" for recollection—who, why and what—are essential as we commune with God. Which one or ones do you find most challenging?

Prayer

Holy God, Jesus my love, Holy Spirit, I long to know you more deeply, love you more completely. Put me in your school of prayer and lead me ever so persistently before your throne of grace. I am just a humble traveler, trusting totally in your generosity, with my eyes on you.

Continue this prayer with your own words.

THE SECOND KEY

SCRIPTURE AND SPIRITUAL READING

You shall put these words of mine in your heart and soul....
Teach them to your children, talking about them when you are
at home and when you are away, when you lie down
and when you rise.

—DEUTERONOMY 11:18-19

God's word in Scripture is nothing less than his mercy manifest in written form. It is a chronicle of his relationship with
humanity from creation through redemption and into the early
years of the church: Scripture is one long declaration of love and
forgiveness from our merciful God.

For too many years Catholics labored under the false impression that a person had to be a Scripture scholar in order to read
and understand the Bible. Fortunately those years are behind us
and with the steady encouragement of our Holy Father, Catholics
have turned in great numbers to reading Scripture. Catholic publishers have responded to this upsurge in interest, presenting us
with a wide selection of Bible studies for group or individual use,

arranged under books of the Bible such as the Psalms or the Gospel of Matthew, as well as under topics, such as virtue or perseverance. There is also plenty of introductory material such as George Martin's book *Reading Scripture as the Word of God* that will help develop a Scripture study habit. See the resource section at the end of this book for more suggestions.

Reading and studying Scripture is essential if you intend to be a faithful and effective Christian. Understanding the history, culture and context for the events in the Bible will enrich and enliven your faith and reveal God's constant presence throughout history, from the beginning to the present. In fact, familiarity with Scripture is food for your journey through life, the daily meal you need in order to grow in your faith.

Read Regularly

It is best if you can read and study the Bible daily, but if that's not possible try to set aside at least fifteen minutes several times a week for Scripture. To help you toward that goal, you can listen to Bible tapes in the car or carry Scripture in your briefcase or purse and read it while you wait for a child's soccer practice to end, a plane or train to arrive, or in any of the empty gaps that pop up in daily life.

Memorizing passages from Scripture can also be very sustaining, giving you a permanent word from the Lord to help you when traveling, tempted, worried or anxious. My husband does this and has found these passages spring to mind just when he needs them. In particular, he has found great strength in hard times in one of his favorite passages:

> I have been crucified with Christ; and it is no longer I who live, but it is Christ who lives in me. And the life I now live in the flesh I live by faith in the Son of God, who loved me and gave himself for me.
>
> —GALATIANS 2:19-20

As you become acquainted with God's Word, you will not only

gain insight into his plan of salvation, you will also find him speaking to you personally through your study.

I once counseled a woman named Margie who had had an abortion as a teenager. She was now a Christian wife and the mother of three. Although she had repented numerous times for the abortion, she still felt guilty and condemned, unable to draw near to God.

After some discussion, she repented of the abortion one last time and agreed that she *never* had to repent of it again because God forgives generously when we bring our sin to him. Then Margie did a Bible study on God's forgiveness and wrote pertinent individual passages on index cards. Whenever guilt raised its head, she read the cards until she felt she knew the truth again. She was able to move forward in her Christian life because she decided to believe Scripture concerning the truth of God's love and forgiveness.

Sometimes Christians shy away from studying biblical history and culture because they fear the information will be too complicated or will divert their attention from the spiritual truths in the Bible, diluting their faith. But Scripture study enhances faith.

Even a simple footnote can help us better appreciate the nuances of a passage. Consider, for example, just one footnote in the story of Jesus' encounter with the Samaritan woman at the well.

The Pharisees heard that Jesus was gaining and baptizing more disciples than John, although in fact it was not Jesus who baptized, but his disciples. When the Lord learned of this, he left Judea and went back once more to Galilee.

> Now he had to go through Samaria. So he came to a town in Samaria called Sychar, near the plot of ground Jacob had given to his son Joseph.
>
> —JOHN 4:4-5 (NIV)

In the NIV Bible, the footnote for verse 4 refers to Samaria and the phrase "had to go" as follows: "*...had to go.* The necessity lay in Jesus' mission, not in geography. *Samaria.* Here, the whole region, not simply the city. Jews often avoided Samaria by crossing the Jordan and traveling on the east side."

This commentary changed the way I read that passage. It was not random circumstance that brought Jesus to Samaria and to that well. He could have gone around Samaria but he had a date with destiny—an opportunity to further his mission of bringing the gospel to all humankind, not just the Jews. This encounter came about not because Jesus developed a thirst en route to Galilee but because the Creator was at work, designing this "chance" meeting.

If we fail to devote time to a more focused study of Scripture, we'll miss much of its riches. For example, images and metaphors that run through the Old and the New Testament—light and darkness, birth and death, floods and rainbows, hiding and finding, Jesus as the "second Adam"—might escape our attention.

But a commentary or Bible study can help us grasp the intimate connection between, say, the Garden of Eden and the Garden of Gethsemane. The sin and rebellion against God in the Garden of Eden was the catalyst that set into motion the suffering of Jesus, the Son of God, in the Garden of Gethsemane. Disobedience reigned in the first Garden; obedience—Jesus' submission to the Father—reigned in the second Garden.

Spiritual, theological, intellectual and historical insights gleaned from studying the Bible will encourage your understanding of God's plan of salvation. Approach your study in a prayerful attitude and God will reveal himself through faith enhanced by reason.

Take It Personally

Sometimes God speaks to us very informally but specifically through Scripture. I remember a day a few years ago when I sat with my Bible on my lap, as I stared out the dining room window at the gray sky. The trees danced about in the wind but my old sweater kept me warm from the October chill. I was in an introspective mood, questioning if I was truly living my life the way God intended. Would he say to me at the pearly gates, "Well done, good and faithful servant"? Or would he say, "Well, on a scale of one to ten, your life was a five." "How *does* one know how to live?" I asked myself. "What is a life truly pleasing to God?" I paged through my Bible absentmindedly, not really expecting to find any answers. Then I noticed passages of Scripture that I had underlined over the years, some of them accompanied by a date and a few words of comment. I began to read these highlighted texts, sometimes remembering clearly, sometimes dimly, the circumstances that had led me to underline the passages.

May 3, 1983, stood in faded ink next to Psalm 116. I remembered the terror and the joy of that day when our daughter Rebecca was born. As an ambulance rushed me to the hospital, sirens screaming, emergency medical technicians attached an IV and heart monitors to my body. This was my fifth child, but my labor had gone terribly wrong. My doctor, with me in the ambulance, could no longer hear the baby's heartbeat and I was having one unrelenting, continuous contraction. My blood pressure was rising dangerously, and I had a splitting headache.

My obstetrician was a Christian who prayed over me as the ambulance raced across town. A friend contacted my husband and followed the ambulance in her car. Not knowing what the outcome would be for my unborn child or me, I offered both of our lives to Jesus, our Savior. At the hospital, as the staff gave me anesthesia in preparation for an emergency Caesarean section, I knew that this could be the last time I closed my eyes on earth.

But Rebecca was born with more healthy vital signs than anyone could have hoped for. I was tired and had some residual paralysis that resolved itself in a few days. I was sore but fine. That day I lifted my heart to God and asked him for a word to give meaning to what had just happened. I prayed and opened my Bible at random to hear the voice of God to me, his comfort after the shock of surgery. The Bible fell open at Psalm 116:

> I love the Lord, for he heard my voice;
>> he heard my cry for mercy.
> Because he turned his ear to me.
>> I will call on him as long as I live.
>
> . . .
>
> The LORD is gracious and righteous;
>> our God is full of compassion.
> The LORD protects the simplehearted;
>> when I was in great need, he saved me.
>
> Be at rest once more, O my soul,
>> for the LORD has been good to you.
> For you, O LORD, have delivereth my soul from death,
>> my eyes from tears,
>> my feet from stumbling,
> that I may walk before the LORD
>> in the land of the living.
>
> —PSALM 116:1-2, 5-9 (NIV)

I was in awe that words written thousands of years ago were the very words that comforted me after a traumatic childbirth in 1983. Each word of the psalm spoke personally to me, like a love letter from God.

Years later on that gray October day, the bright light of truth pierced my thoughts. As I once again cherished these words in Scripture, the gentle light of Christ reminded me that God had spoken to me and guided me in the past and would continue to do so in the future. I had let the mist of doubt swirl around my thoughts, forgetting God's goodness to me. But as he spoke to me through Scripture, his Word sustained me on my journey home.

This sort of informal or random opening of the Scripture,

used sparingly, can be helpful in the life of the Christian. Even the saints occasionally approached Scripture this way. For example, prior to receiving the stigmata—the five wounds of Christ that sometimes appear on the bodies of great saints—St. Francis had an intimation that God was about to act powerfully in his life. He had one of his friars open the gospel at random three times and each time, it fell open at the Passion of Jesus. He understood then that soon he would enter more deeply into the sufferings of Christ.

The dangers with this approach to Scripture are fairly obvious. Don't use the Bible for fortune-telling! But God can and sometimes does minister to us in this way, as a supplement to his feeding of us through daily familiarity with his Word.

Spiritual Reading
Most Christians benefit from reading other spiritual books in addition to the Bible. These might include history, biography, autobiography and fiction by Christian authors.

Lives of the Saints. Lives of the saints are popular because we can identify with these men and women as they struggled to become more like Christ. St. Augustine, for example, lived an indulgent life before his dramatic conversion. His mother, St. Monica, interceded relentlessly for him and is an inspiration to many parents whose children have abandoned the values they were taught at home. Augustine credited his conversion to his mother's determined intercession.

Christian Self-help. Books devoted to other aspects of life such as prayer, healing, forgiveness, men's and women's issues, Christian parenting, Christian marriage and so on can also strengthen us in our Christian walk. In my clinical practice, I facilitate healing by recommending books that expand on what the client and I discuss in our sessions, trusting the Holy Spirit both to help me match the person with the right book and to inspire the person as they read the book.

Finding help with personal issues through reading can be tremendously effective. Rather than merely picking the hottest bestseller off the shelf, though, look for a book that addresses your need from a Christian perspective. A religious bookstore is a good place to find a spiritual approach to dealing with everything from relationship issues to addiction to financial difficulties.

Autobiography. Some books are just absorbing or fun or heartrending to read as they reveal eternal truths. *A Severe Mercy,* Sheldon Vanauken's autobiography, had a profound effect on me. This author and his wife had an intense and disordered romantic love that was redeemed by the transforming love of Jesus prior to the wife's illness and untimely death.

Even best-sellers for the secular market can have powerful spiritual themes—a strong spirituality is not uncommon in the lives of those who rise to prominence. See if there are books available by people whose spirituality you admire. It can be very enlightening to see the many ways one can live an authentic Christian life.

Fiction. I find many of C.S. Lewis's books to be compelling and life-changing but my family and I have been especially captivated by *The Chronicles of Narnia*, a series of books featuring the lion Aslan, a Christ-figure. In one of the early *Narnia* books, one of the children is told to watch for three signs—they were important. Of course, he forgets the signs or remembers them incorrectly at first. My husband and I know that God has given us certain important guidelines or signs for our lives that we need to remember for our journey. One is the simple and powerful truth: "Our lives are in his hands." We gently remind each other to not forget the signs for our adventure. When we fail to remember and speak of these truths, we become anxious or frustrated.

Periodicals. Finally, we can find spiritual sustenance in daily devotionals organized according to the calendar or liturgical seasons. Magazines such as *Magnificat* and *The Word Among Us,* representative of this genre, deliver spiritual support in bite-size pieces. A subscription to a solid, general-interest Catholic magazine can keep you abreast of the Church's view on current events.

For Reflection

Do you hesitate to read the Bible? It is God's love letter to you, so open it and ask the Lord to speak to your heart. Write here about the Scripture that you are reading. What is the Lord saying to you through his timeless Word? Remember that he speaks justice, mercy and love.

Ask your friends what spiritual reading they have found inspiring and helpful. Check out bookstores or Web sites for books about spiritual topics that interest you.

Consider subscribing to a periodical with a spiritual theme. It will be a monthly or weekly reminder to do a spiritual check-up, and it may bring faith issues to your attention that might otherwise have gone unnoticed.

Prayer

Jesus, I long to know and love you more. Teach me more about yourself through your life-giving Word. Lead me to the books of Scripture and inspired writings that will expand my knowledge and insight into the spiritual life. Help me to hear your message for my life.

Continue this prayer in your own words.

THE THIRD KEY

THE SACRAMENTS

For as the heavens are high above the earth,
so great is his steadfast love toward those who fear him;
as far as the east is from the west,
so far he removes our transgressions from us.
As a father has compassion for his children,
so the LORD has compassion for those who fear him.

PSALM 103:11-13

The seven sacraments are a lifeline to heaven, a rich source of grace and mercy. It is our privilege as Catholics to have these gifts of the church available for our use. A thorough understanding of each sacrament can lead to a deeper appreciation of the life we have in Christ.

Baptism

Baptism is the birth of the Christian. Whether you were baptized as an infant or later in life, it signaled the beginning of your life in Christ. If you cannot remember the day of your baptism, try to recreate it in your imagination—your parents and godparents, the Church and its baptismal font, the clothing your wore, the words that were said. The baptismal rite begins with a critical question, "What do you ask of God's Church?" The ritual of the sacrament also enlists us in the important work of the Christian to wage war in the spiritual battle between the kingdom of light and the kingdom of darkness: "Do you reject Satan?"

With infant baptism, the Catholic Church recognizes the need for sacramental grace as soon as a little life comes into the world. Parents say yes to faith on behalf of their child but all of us, as members of the church and the community of believers, can affirm our own yes each day by making decisions that will strengthen us personally and the church through us. Each sin or failing of ours is an injury to this Body—one that must be healed as soon as possible. Each act of faith or goodness strengthens us and strengthens Christ's presence on earth. If we begin each day by choosing anew to be Christian—to embrace the joys and trials of that choice—we'll find the help to live out our baptismal commitment.

The Holy Eucharist

When Jesus introduced the Eucharist to his disciples it created quite a reaction. In fact, for some this was the "deal breaker" for their relationship with Jesus. Read and meditate on this important passage:

> Jesus said to them, "Very truly, I tell you, unless you eat the flesh of the Son of Man and drink his blood, you have no life in you. Those who eat my flesh and drink my blood have eternal life, and I will raise them up on the last day; for my flesh is true food and my blood is true drink. Those who eat my flesh and drink my blood abide in me, and I in them." ... When many of his disciples heard it, they said, "This teaching is difficult; who

can accept it?"...Because of this, many of his disciples turned back and no longer went about with him.

—JOHN 6:53-56, 60, 66

The Catholic church describes this Eucharistic reality as *transub-stantiation*, meaning that the bread at the moment of consecration becomes Jesus' flesh and the wine becomes his blood: the inner reality or essence becomes the flesh and blood of Jesus even though the appearance, the bread and wine, does not change. We believe this on faith. This truth is the reason why Catholics have such reverence for the Eucharist: It is no less than Jesus himself, present to us, body and blood.

Don't make the mistake of confusing faith with feelings. You don't need to *feel* that the host is the body of Christ. Just act on it, accept this ancient article of faith, and receive Jesus himself in the Eucharist, daily if possible. This will be an incredible source of grace and blessing for you.

It will also be an opportunity for the sort of healing and strengthening we all need in order to carry on with our lives. During the liturgy of the Eucharist, the priest takes the host, raises it slightly and, facing the congregation, says, "This is the Lamb of God who takes away the sins of the world. Happy are those who are called to his supper." We respond, "Lord, I am not worthy to receive you, but only say the word and I shall be healed." Frequently in Scripture the Lord uses the concepts of healing and forgiveness interchangeably. Here in the Eucharist we will find the daily and usual means of that healing, spiritually, emotionally and physically.

At one point in my life when I felt far from my Lord, I decided to be spiritually assertive and go to daily Mass and Communion despite my lack of felt faith. As I look back on that time, I see that my decision was a turning point in my spiritual life. Receiving Jesus in the Eucharist is always a win-win situation. Making the space in your life to do this is worth it.

St. Gemma, who lived in the late 1800s and is one of the patron saints of the Eucharist, received Communion daily. She suffered very dark, dry, spiritual times in her life but the Lord often spoke to her heart when she received the Eucharist. I imagine that he speaks to all of our hearts when we receive Communion, but we are not as spiritually sensitive as young Gemma.

Weekly Mass is an obligation for Catholics, but any good relationship depends on going beyond what is required. If daily Mass is not a possibility for you, attend as often as you can. Do not miss an opportunity to receive Communion when you are able.

Reconciliation

A friend of mine who converted to Catholicism had a life-changing experience with the sacrament of reconciliation. Pete's dad was in the army and so, when Pete was young, his family moved around the world, attending whatever church was most convenient, from Methodist to Pentecostal.

Pete was raised to understand confession of sin as a very private affair between God and him without the need for any third party. But he was not sure. He often read Scripture passages referring to God's generosity in forgiving since he suffered frequent doubt that he was forgiven.

Over the years, he found himself working with colleagues who were Catholics. One coworker invited Pete to morning Mass while they were traveling on business. Pete thought it probably couldn't hurt since he hadn't reconnected with a church as an adult.

He asked about the sacraments, was intrigued with the universality of the Catholic Church, and eventually decided to become a Catholic. He prepared for his first confession and although he was uncomfortable telling his sins to a priest, he went ahead and did it. In a powerful moment of sacramental grace, Pete actually felt a physical heaviness lift from him as the priest said the prayers of absolution. The knowledge that Christ indeed saw his sins from the cross and forgave him replaced the spiritual and psychological torment Pete suffered from guilt. This sacrament brought peace and joy in place of guilt and shame to Pete's heart.

As all Catholics know, the priest is the representative of Jesus in the confessional. There is no need to feel self-conscious when you confess to the priest because Jesus knows your sins already and forgives you as you bring them to him. This is why he died on the cross. Further, when you confess and receive absolution, your sins are wiped clean. The analogy of the school chalkboard can be useful here. I remember clearing the school chalkboard with erasers at the end of a school day. A white residue remained but on Friday afternoons a couple of students *washed* the blackboard. The difference was incredible. The white residue disappeared and the board was clean. This is the way our souls are after the sacrament of reconciliation: wiped clean as if there were never any sin. Also, the grace of the sacrament strengthens us to avoid sin in the future.

Enlightening the Mind. In order to fully appreciate the sacrament of reconciliation, Christians need to understand some basic facts about the nature of sin. One of many challenges facing us in the early stages of the journey to heaven is learning a new way of thinking: we must enlighten our mind and turn from sin. In Paul's letter to the Ephesians, he addresses this important issue:

> You were taught to put away your former way of life, your old self, corrupt and deluded by its lusts, and to be renewed in the spirit of your minds, and to clothe yourselves with the new self, created according to the likeness of God in true righteousness and holiness.
>
> —EPHESIANS 4:22-24

Conversion implies a change from one thing to another. Much of the change from pre-conversion darkness to post-conversion light occurs on the battleground of our mind. It is here, in the mind, that the war between the kingdom of light and the kingdom of darkness takes place.

Conversion, the *Catechism of the Catholic Church* points out, "requires convincing of sin" (*CCC*, #1848), and the turning of our lives and hearts toward the light and the love of Christ. Many well-intentioned people are confused about this point of sin. Some argue that what they think is sin may not be the same as another person's understanding of sin. How true! That is why Christians must conform their standards for love and holiness to God's standards. He defines the objective moral and ethical boundaries, not us. He gave us the Ten Commandments, not the Ten Suggestions.

Sin is not just about behavior: if it were, stopping the behavior would be all that is required. Sin is actually a symptom of living independently of the will of God. In order to live by his will, however, our minds and hearts need to be informed and formed by objective truth as presented in Scripture and the teachings of the church.

Unfortunately, both new and secularized Christians often approach issues of right and wrong from a subjective or relativistic stance.

A *subjective* approach to right and wrong allows each person to decide for himself what is good. This reasoning has its roots in an atheistic understanding of the universe. Since there is no God or Creator and therefore no "owner's manual" to live by, then individuals can judge for themselves. "I won't tell you what to do," the thinking goes, "and you won't tell me what to do."

Relativity is based on the belief that moral or ethical judgments may be different—therefore relative—to any given set of circumstances. For example, a relativist might argue that abortion for convenience is wrong but if rape or incest is involved it is OK. With this reasoning, the question of right or wrong shifts to an emotional appeal based on empathy for the woman. Empathy is appropriate and absolutely the Christian response to a woman in this situation. However, abortion is wrong based on the moral precept that all murder is wrong. We cannot trade the life of a child for empathy for a woman. They are not mutually exclusive categories; we can demonstrate tremendous empathy while safeguarding life.

Both approaches, of course, can let us skew a situation to satisfy our own inclinations, as happened years ago with my own children. As I stood at the kitchen sink one summer day, I saw my daughter Cathy, then five years old, dragging her three-year-old sister to the kitchen door. Rebecca was crying loudly, but I was able to make out the words " . . . but I didn't *know*!" Cathy, in a manner that only older sisters can master, said to me "Mom, Rebecca just broke one of the commandments." I couldn't imagine what commandment Rebecca had managed to break in our sandbox.

"Which commandment?" I asked as I wiped Rebecca's tears. "You know, Mom. The one that says 'You shall obey your mother, your father and your older sister!'"

Subjectivity and relativity are flawed but popular decision-making methods. Too often, our natural inclinations are in conflict with our faith. We fall into error, choosing wrong behavior and justifying it through subjective or relativistic rationalizations.

Jason and Holly, age sixteen, attended the same Christian youth conference where they both welcomed Jesus into their lives. Beginning that weekend and for many weeks after, Jason and Holly prayed and talked together daily about what the Lord was teaching them and about details of their personal lives. What began as "brother and sister in the Lord" evolved into emotional and sexual intensity. One evening after praying in the chapel, they "knew" they were "spiritually married" and proceeded to consummate their marriage later that night.

This young couple's plight is an example of both subjectivity and relativity: they chose to rely of their own judgment of right and wrong without measuring it against the Word of God, and they judged themselves exempt from the commandments due to their spiritual marriage. It is just such subjective, emotional thinking that creates obstacles for the growing Christian.

Guilt and shame need never be obstacles for Catholics in their relationship with God. Challenge yourself to receive the sacrament of reconciliation more frequently. The grace of reconciliation coupled with frequent reception of the Eucharist will keep you grounded and able to withstand the storms and troubles of daily life.

Confirmation

Many Catholics think of confirmation as making them "soldiers for Christ." Confirmation is a sacrament of spiritual maturity. It strengthens us with the Holy Spirit, preparing us for the obstacles and challenges of adult life.

I received the sacrament of confirmation in eighth grade. I remember that as I prepared for this moment I really expected the sacrament to bring about a change in my life. I was going to receive the Third Person of the Trinity and as the Spirit came to me, I would be joining the army of God. When the big day came, I solemnly processed up the aisle to where the bishop stood. I was ready for the encounter of a lifetime.

The bishop said the prayers and when he tapped my cheek as a sign of my willingness to suffer for my faith, he used his hand to push me along so the next person could step forward. Needless to say, I was disappointed.

After the church service ended and the family party was over, I felt foolish for thinking something would happen. Since then, I've heard many Catholics say quite strongly that the power of the Holy Spirit attested to in the Acts of the Apostles was meant for the early church, but not for now. They needed that power back then, the thinking goes, but we don't today. My own experience at confirmation not only seemed to confirm that, it also planted within me the seeds of low expectations for my life with God.

The problem, of course, is not with the Holy Spirit. Nevertheless, I think my disappointment and confusion at the age of fourteen is typical. Like so many, I had no one to help me understand the action of the Holy Spirit in my life.

I wish someone had told me that after God sent his son to live among us, to die on the cross, and to be raised from the dead for us, his action didn't end. When Jesus returned to heaven, God sent the Holy Spirit to be with us until the end of time.

This is exciting news, too often overlooked. God doesn't tell humanity, "Well, I've done my part; you're on your own now." He gives us an advocate and defender—his own Holy Spirit—who is actually within each of us. Jesus continues:

> I have said these things to you while I am still with you. But the Advocate, the Holy Spirit, whom the Father will send in my name, will teach you everything, and remind you of all that I have said to you.
>
> —JOHN 14:25-26

According to the plan of the Trinity, the Spirit will not only come and live within us, the Spirit will then teach us about and remind us of the things of God. This is the complete plan of action God promises to every Christian.

As we know, this plan was fulfilled at Pentecost when God poured out his Spirit on the disciples. Prior to his Ascension, Jesus ordered his disciples "not to leave Jerusalem, but to wait there for the promise of the Father...for John baptized with water, but you will be baptized with the Holy Spirit" (Acts 1:4-5).

This promise was intended for all of us, for all time. Jesus gives no indication that the Spirit is coming just to the early Christians in order to help them establish the church. And yet many people feel that since the church is established, we no longer need the Spirit's powerful action. But if today is not a good time for the Holy Spirit to come in power, when is? We only have to read the headlines to recognize that the world needs the Spirit now more than ever. True, Christianity is a major world religion. But the evidence of hearts converted to Christ is disproportionately low when compared to statistics regarding the number of Christians worldwide.

The Work of the Holy Spirit Today. The good news is that we already have the Holy Spirit within us through the sacraments of baptism and confirmation. When we ask him to fill our lives with himself, we will begin to grow in appreciation for and reliance on him.

As we all learned at confirmation, the Spirit also brings various gifts such as wisdom, counsel, fear of the Lord and knowledge (Is 11:2) as well as discernment of spirits, prophecy, healing and so on (1 Cor 12:4-11).

God bestows these gifts through the sacraments and also through our asking for them to be made manifest. This manifestation of God's gifts should flow regularly through our lives in very real ways. For example, in the course of my work I recently saw a specific manifestation of the gift of wisdom.

Another counselor called me one afternoon to discuss a difficult and complex case. A client was in significant emotional pain but months of therapy had yielded little relief. (Therapists sometimes seek peer counsel when necessary.) I knew that this counselor was a Christian and after discussing different approaches and insights, I suggested she pray and ask the Holy Spirit for the gifts of wisdom and knowledge.

Several weeks later, she called me with wonderful news. She had prayed for the spiritual gifts of wisdom and knowledge and, as always, the Holy Spirit gave generously. My colleague experienced promptings of the Spirit and insights that could have only been supernatural. These gifts of love from the Holy Spirit brought a degree of healing that no therapy could have achieved.

This active presence of the Holy Spirit should be the standard experience of normal Christian life. We were designed this way. Let me share a very practical analogy from my own life.

Several Christmases ago, we bought a high-end vacuum cleaner after years of buying lower-end models that needed to be replaced every two years. (I'm sure our gang of five, plus cats and dogs, helped achieved that high turnover.) The first time I used the vacuum, I tried to forget how much we spent on it and turned it on expecting great things. It picked up the dirt but it was so heavy that I had to drag it back and forth on the carpet. It was considerably more work than I'd had with my old one.

When I complained to my husband that night, he checked it and discovered that I hadn't turned on the power drive for the machine. I had been wasting energy dragging this vacuum around the living room; if I had pushed the power button, it would have glided along with little effort on my part.

Living the Christian life without the fullness of the Holy Spirit is like failing to turn on the power drive. We were designed to live in his power.

Make sure that you are taking full advantage of the power of the Holy Spirit in your life. As a baptized, confirmed Catholic, you already have this power available to you. Just make sure you turn it on.

Marriage

I recently took a class with a sociology professor who pointed out that the family is the "basic unit and building block of society." The social sciences value marriage as integral to the stability of the larger human community but our Christian understanding of marriage goes well beyond that to achieve a depth and complexity in the very heart of God.

Marriage shares some aspects of the sacraments of baptism and confirmation—it is received in community and a decided *yes* is required. To choose marriage is to choose a high and demanding vocation within the church. It is unique: the union of man and woman reflects the union and the love of the Blessed Trinity, the mysterious giving and receiving of love continuously at work among the three divine persons. That circle of infinite love bursts forth not only in the creation of the physical universe but also in the creation of humanity, made in the image of this Holy Trinity.

Those who enter into marriage share the creative aspect of that Divine Love, conceiving and giving life to another human being. Childbirth, the most common of events, is truly humbling and awe-inspiring when seen in the light of divine creation.

A sacramental understanding of marriage helps put in perspective the intense and insidious assault on marriage today. Communication problems, compatibility problems or "irreconcilable" differences are, in truth, the human expression of the war waged between the two kingdoms. Since marriage is an image of the Trinity, of God's faithfulness, of his unconditional love, it should not surprise us that the evil one wants to destroy it.

Holy Orders

Holy orders is the other "vocation" sacrament. Jesus knew that a commitment to be his disciple was a costly one. In the priesthood, the church offers Christian men the opportunity to express their love for Christ by choosing to lay down their lives for God's people. In doing so, they forgo the vocation of marriage. Although this sacrament requires a tremendous sacrifice on the part of those who say yes, holy orders shares in the same communal nature that characterizes the sacrament of marriage. In their yes to Jesus Christ, priests enter into a relationship with the Trinity as intensely committed as the relationship between husband and wife. (See the *Catechism of the Catholic Church*, #1569-1571, for a discussion of the diaconate and holy orders.)

Christian history is filled with great men who served the church unstintingly, often with little earthly reward. St. John Neumann, the bishop of Philadelphia, once said: "My only consolation is the piety of the faithful of the diocese. Everything else is fear, hardship and work." We must pray for the priests who serve us, and that more good and holy men choose this blessed path to union with God and service of his people.

Anointing of the Sick

Catholics are blessed to have the sacrament of the anointing of the sick. Formerly, this sacrament was reserved for the dying but is now offered to the seriously ill as well. Recently I attended morning Mass in our parish when the pastor explained that a parishioner had been diagnosed with a potentially life-threatening illness and was having surgery the next day. That person was present and at the end of the liturgy the pastor invited him and anyone else with a serious medical condition to come forward for prayer and anointing with sacramental oil.

As well as being an opportunity for healing, this sacrament imparts the peace and courage of the Holy Spirit. I was relieved and grateful that when both my dad and my father-in-law were dying, there was a priest willing to come to their bedsides to administer the love and forgiveness of Christ at the hour of their death. This sacrament, which can be received more than once, prepares us for that final journey home to the Lord.

For Reflection

What steps can you take today to increase your understanding of these gifts from God? Ask the Lord to lead you to books about the sacraments or to opportunities to share with Catholic friends about the sacraments.

Sometimes our internal restlessness is due to spiritual hunger. If you receive the body of Christ once a week at Sunday Mass, that's wonderful! Consider going to Mass and confession at least one more time than you usually do. List the intentions that you would like to offer up at this extra Mass when receiving the body of our Lord, Jesus Christ.

When you attend the wedding of a friend, or the first communion of a relative, be mindful of the importance of the spiritual depth of these sacraments. How can you keep yourself and others more conscious of the sacred nature of these occasions?

Prayer

Jesus, inspire me to receive the sacraments more frequently. Help me to remember my dignity as a Christian and to take the responsibilities of

Christian life seriously. Show me how I can deepen my relationship with you by changing how I approach reconciliation or Eucharist.

Continue this prayer in your own words.

THE FOURTH KEY

COMMUNITY

For in the one Spirit we were all baptized into one body
—Jews or Greeks, slaves or free—and we were all made
to drink of one Spirit.... Now you are the body of Christ
and individually members of it.

—1 CORINTHIANS 12:13, 27

The Trinity, the perfect communion of Father, Son and Spirit, is always the starting point in our understanding of community.

Community can be expressed in many ways but the image of the cross captures the essential relationships in the Christian life. The vertical beam of the cross that held our Lord's bleeding head and feet is symbolic of God's relationship with us, and his love flowing to us. The horizontal beam of the cross, the wood to which Christ's hands were nailed, symbolizes the flow of divine love through us to the rest of the world.

The Church came into being when Jesus died for us and, soon after, the Spirit descended upon the disciples at Pentecost. This Church is the body of Christ not only spiritually but tangibly: it consists of men, women and children of every race, height, weight, age, and personality type. These are our brothers and sisters: we are all designed by our creator to receive his love through one another, not just through private prayer.

Christ came to redeem us, to forgive us, and to give us life everlasting. He also came to teach us how to live together as his body until his return on the last day. He has equipped us for that because the redeeming love that flowed from Jesus on the cross still flows through his body, the Church, today.

Faith and Action

Sometimes it's hard to admit, but we need to share our faith, joys, sorrows, and daily struggles with other believers. The unifying action of shared faith brings friends and strangers together in understanding and encouragement.

The story of the rebuilding of Jerusalem after the Babylonian captivity of the Jews illustrates this truth. The pagans who occupied Jerusalem in the absence of the Jews destroyed the Temple and the walls of the city. These gentiles didn't want the walls (which protected the Jews) or the Temple (their holy place of worship and the center of their faith) rebuilt. If the Jews succeeded in rebuilding, they would regain their power as an independent nation.

Nehemiah, a layman, led his fellow Jews in the task of restoration. As the gaps in the walls began to close, Israel's enemies took up arms to prevent their success. Nehemiah reports:

> ...all plotted together to come and fight against Jerusalem and to cause confusion in it. So we prayed to our God, and set a guard as a protection against them day and night....From that day on, half of my servants worked on construction, and half held the spears, shields, bows and body-armor; and the leaders posted themselves behind the whole house of Judah, who were building the wall. The burden bearers carried their loads

in such a way that each labored on the work with one hand and with the other held a weapon.

—NEHEMIAH 4:8-9, 16-18

The NIV translation of the Bible has a footnote to verses 8-9: "Prayer and watchfulness blend faith and action, and also emphasize both the divine side and the human side."

And so it is with the body of Christ. The image of the people of God keeping each other safe, day and night, is powerful. The body of believers is itself a sort of spiritual battle plan. When one Christian feels besieged by discouragement, illness, or the pressures of daily life, his brothers and sisters in Christ can pray for him and provide personal support while he is under fire. Like the Israelites building the wall, one builds while another stands guard and keeps him safe.

Expressions of Community

We find this type of support in many places, particularly the church, where we receive teaching, spiritual direction, and sacramental grace. Groups that meet for Bible study, prayer, discussion or support also provide Christians with opportunities for personal encouragement and growth.

And we should never underestimate the impact of casual or apparently random encounters that unexpectedly offer powerful support. I remember flying cross-country one evening as the flight attendants, while cleaning up from dinner (or was it pretzels?), dimmed the cabin lights. I was tired and had avoided praying or reading my Bible for no other reason than that I didn't feel like it. Having an aisle seat gave me a view of the seats on either side of the aisle ahead of me. One flight attendant patiently collected trash, finished cleaning up, and then refilled coffee cups. Finally she sat down two rows ahead of me. Not realizing that she was observed, she sighed deeply, wiped her face with both hands, and reached into her bag. "Now that woman has a right to be tired," I thought. She deserved a few minutes relaxation. Then I saw her draw her Bible from the bag, place it on her lap, find the black ribbon that marked her place, and begin to read. Within minutes a nearby passenger asked for water and she quietly returned the Bible to her bag and met the request. This encounter with another Christian convicted me of my laziness. She testified, strengthened and encouraged me without ever knowing it.

The Community of Marriage. It may be strange to think of a community of two, but that is what a marriage is. A successful marriage will have its foundation in eternal principles, rather than passing circumstances of attraction, or employment, or living conditions, or financial or health concerns.

Randy and I have been married for thirty-four years. Our relationship began the summer of my conversion; from the beginning I saw Randy as a son of God and he saw me as a daughter of God. In a very real way, this made us brother and sister in Christ. This understanding—that we are brother and sister in Christ, called to treat one another as a son or daughter of God—is the foundation for our deep love. As we travel through life together, we often tell one another how blessed we are to have that firm foundation. Nothing else could have secured our profound unity in the face of all the normal marital tensions and the trials and troubles of life.

The Community of Family. The family, of course, is one of the most natural settings in which to establish each other in Jesus and his ways. Husbands and wives help each other make time to pray or get to Mass. They raise children in the faith, discipline them, and teach them virtue. Not all families are this "domestic church" (as the *Catechism* describes it, #1658) but this is still the place where we have tremendous opportunity to die to ourselves, love and serve others, and receive no thanks—just as Jesus often receives no thanks!

I am in community with my husband and family. Randy and

I share love, concern and prayer for our adult children, their spouses and our grandchild. We have dedicated our family to the Sacred Heart of Jesus, displaying a picture of Jesus and his Sacred Heart in our home and placing our home and everyone in the family in his saving care. We renew this devotion when the family gathers on the holidays. We hope that our children will continue to dedicate their families to his love.

For some years our family had single young adults living with us. This served a dual purpose. It provided practical support to my husband and me as we served the church while raising five children. At the same time, this arrangement provided the young adults with the experience of living in a Christian family while receiving guidance and support from Randy and me.

I am also blessed that my five siblings are all men and women of faith. At family holidays we pray and thank the Lord for what he is doing in our family, for ailing parents, or kids in crisis. We regularly e-mail and phone each other with prayer requests.

The Community of the Church. When we have had family crises over the years, the Christian community, the body of Christ, met our needs: they put our requests on telephone prayer chains, brought dinners, and sent cards encouraging us in the Lord. People invited our children to their homes and entertained and fed them while we handled the adult concerns of illness or death. I encourage you not to miss out on the richness of community life within the church. You don't have to attend every fish fry or parish fundraiser, but don't be a stranger to your church. Sunday Mass is the minimum. Consider dropping by during the week for a few moments of prayer. Join a Bible study. Teach a religious education class. Get involved and stay involved.

At times a community of believers—a parish, a prayer group, a faith-sharing group—can experience hardship and stress. This is normal and no cause to give up. Randy and I were once in a prayer group that was facing serious difficulty. We handled it by getting together with three other couples once a month to pray, snack and play some games. As things settled down and the

crisis passed, we met less frequently. But our instinct—to nour-
ish ourselves spiritually, physically and with a good dose of
humor—provided a crucial lifeline at a critical time in our lives.

The Local Community. In a variety of ways Jesus told us to "do the
works that I do," perhaps most vividly when washing the apos-
tle's feet at the Last Supper.

> If I, your Lord and Teacher, have washed your feet, you
> also ought to wash one another's feet. For I have set you
> an example, that you also should do as I have done to you.
> —JOHN 13:14-15

What is the work that Jesus is doing? He is showing us the
Kingdom of God, designed for sinners who reach out for a savior. Our part of this mission is to pray for and be alert to establishing that kingdom in imitation of Jesus. And where is our mission field? For most of us, it is in our everyday life—at home, on
the bus, on the beach, at work. When will God call us to act?
Usually when we least expect it. If we are to do this work successfully, prayer must precede evangelism. We must be led by the
Holy Spirit in order to know what is the work of the Father and
to be alert to the promptings of the Holy Spirit.

One day at work, for example, I concluded a session with
Jerry, a middle-aged man. Jerry struggled with severe depression
but was making slow yet unmistakable progress. We set up an
appointment for the next week and for some reason I felt like I
should ask if there was anything else I could do for him that day.
I usually don't ask that question when ending a session. Jerry did-
n't believe in God. When I asked if there was anything else I
could do, he paused, looked directly at me, and said with great
feeling, "Yes. Convince me there is a heaven."

You can imagine my shock. I recovered after a brief moment
and said, "Absolutely. I can do that." Jerry pleaded, "How can you
be so confident?" "Because I know God personally and I will ask
him to bring you to that same knowledge," I replied. After that,

we spent regular time each week sharing Scripture that applied to his life.

This type of everyday evangelism requires a yes from us—yes to Jesus as our Lord, yes to turning from sin, and yes to doing his work here on earth.

Being the Love of Christ

Jesus made caring for the needy a condition for entering the kingdom of heaven. Those who clothe the naked, feed the hungry, and visit the sick and imprisoned not only inherit the kingdom of God, they also serve Jesus who identified himself as the one who is hungry, sick, naked and imprisoned (read Mt 25:31-46). Caring for the poor includes our responsibility as Christians to promote justice in every area of life. This can involve us in efforts ranging from providing medical care and adequate housing for the poor to literally feeding the hungry.

We can do this by working personally with local food kitchens or food distribution centers, or by contributing to national or international efforts to alleviate hunger, build houses or install safe drinking water in impoverished areas. Perhaps, closer to home, we have other opportunities. We don't usually know our neighbor's financial state: maybe neighborhood children who hang around our yard at mealtime are there because they are hungry. Maybe they need clothing or shoes or just an encouraging, welcoming word.

And we should remember that we can bring God's love to one another through prayer for every type of healing. We are all called to be Jesus to one another. Any Christian can confidently lay hands on another person's head or shoulder and ask Jesus to restore health, or pray with another over the phone for healing, or pray in private or during Eucharistic adoration. The power to heal belongs to God, so we don't need to be concerned about our shortcomings. And our prayer should include intercession for emotional needs as well as physical. The hidden wounds of the heart need healing, too.

We should also offer practical support, friendship, and encouragement to the sick. As the Letter of James says,

> If a brother or sister is naked and lacks daily food, and one of you says to them, "Go in peace; keep warm and eat your fill," and yet you do not supply their bodily needs, what is the good of that?

—JAMES 2:15-16

Years ago one of our friends was diagnosed with breast cancer. Only forty-two years old, Mary had six children, and this was her third bout with cancer. Unfortunately, the disease progressed and she was restricted to bed. Since Mary's greatest wish was to be a mother to her children, she chose to set up her bed in the living room, the busiest place in their home.

A group of her friends decided to provide her with twenty-four-hour care so that she and her husband could do parenting "as usual." We were the backup team. This support of the sick and the dying is the usual work of the body of Christ. Were we inconvenienced? Certainly. But who cares about inconvenience when a sister in Christ is about to enter the Kingdom of Heaven?

Nor should we be hesitant about consoling the dying or hold back when we have the opportunity to offer emotional or psychological support. Recently our family experienced the loss of my husband's dad at eighty-three and my dad at ninety-two. The course of illness and old age introduced us to hospitals and nursing homes, an education most of us would rather avoid.

The quality of personal care varies in these institutions; one, which we dealt with briefly, was decorated like a five-star hotel but was woefully understaffed. Patients were moaning and ringing their help bells but getting no response. When my husband and I walked down the hall toward my dad's room, we heard the moans and cries of other residents. We tried to mind our own business but felt drawn to meeting the needs of these souls near the end of their time.

As I was on my way to get ice chips for my dad, I heard a woman call out. I glanced around for either family or staff and then hesitantly went in and told her that I would try to find help for her. She grabbed my hand and held it tight, her seemingly fragile condition belying her strength. This elderly woman earnestly beseeched me to pray for her soul. She knew that she would die soon and had no one to pray for her. I turned the cross on her dresser to make it easier for her to see it from her bed. Then I prayed for her.

Several days later, I passed her room and found the bed empty. The staff told me that she had died the night before. I was humbled: I had been so close to walking past her room. My response to the inspiration of the Holy Spirit was pretty dull when I reluctantly ventured in to help her. My eyes still fill with tears when I realize that I was only marginally sensitive to the promptings of the Holy Spirit that night.

There are so many similar "appointments" with God in our lives. For me, I heard the promptings of the Holy Spirit in the environment of the sick and the dying. Sometimes, though, we don't realize how close to death someone may be. Car accidents, drownings, shootings—these bring the young, the middle-aged, and the healthy to death. Since we never know whom the Lord will call next, our role is to be sensitive to the prompting of the Holy Spirit.

For Reflection

Do pride, self-consciousness or negative past experiences keep you from receiving the love of Christ through others? List the obstacles in your life to receiving that love in the body of Christ.

What does doing the works of God mean to you in your life? Are you called to intercede for others to know the love of Christ? Are you called to get out of your comfort zone and directly share the love, healing and hope of Christ crucified?

Is Jesus calling you to serve the sick and the dying? How?

Prayer

Jesus, I humbly ask you to let me share your ministry to the poor, the hungry, the sick and the dying. Give me the grace to share this work of yours.

Continue this prayer in your own words.

THE FIFTH KEY

VIRTUE

Make me to know your ways, O LORD;
teach me your paths.
Lead me in your truth, and teach me,
for you are the God of my salvation;
for you I wait all day long.

—PSALM 25:4-5

Armed with a cup of coffee for energy and cassette tapes on the life of St. Teresa of Avila for inspiration, I set out for a five-hour drive to visit my parents in Michigan. Dashing to the car, I regretted that I was leaving the house later than I had planned. I promised myself that I would try to make up the time. The morning was perfect with a brilliant blue sky and low humidity; the countryside was bursting with the energy of early spring. It was the sort of day when the sunlight actually looks yellow. The road had dried from the prior evening's rain and traffic was light. I set the cruise control just a bit faster than I usually would, promising myself that I would keep an eye on the rearview mirror for flashing lights. I would save no time if I were stopped for a ticket.

My eyes frequently strayed to that mirror to check for the unwanted presence of the police. I was more than satisfied with the weather and sparse traffic so I indulged myself with glances back to check out a particularly intriguing car, or a restaurant off the highway, or an exit as I zipped by. The guilt of driving faster than the speed limit prompted many a backward glance, too. After one such look into the rearview mirror, I contentedly looked ahead once more.

God, no! I panicked as I saw a sea of red brake lights in front of me. I was closing in on them all too quickly. I slammed on the brakes, my mind frantically seeking a strategy to avoid the black Ford pickup truck immediately in front of me. Could I stop in time?

I felt the tires biting into the pavement as the tail of my car began to swing wide to the right. I was quickly approaching the moment of decision. Should I risk rear-ending the truck, hoping the car would stop in time, or should I drive onto the grass median knowing that there was a good chance that the car could roll as it reached the steep slope?

The car stopped in time but my heart raced, my palms were sweaty, and my legs began to tremble. All of this occurred in a few seconds of real time, but every fraction of those seconds was seared into my brain. I pulled the car off the highway and put my head on the steering wheel, trembling. I had indulged in lingering looks in the rearview mirror and almost killed others and myself.

A few months after that traffic incident, Kelly, a friend, told me that she was once again struggling with a particularly difficult relationship in her life. Kelly had been raised by an alcoholic father who, when sober, was a demanding perfectionist and, when drunk, was verbally and physically violent. That experience affected all subsequent relationships in her life and I reminded her that considering the home environment in which she grew up, I wasn't surprised that she was still struggling with this. After a moment of silence she told me that she was tired of looking at her past to excuse the lack of progress in her life. "I'm sick of going over and over the same insights about how what happened in the past contributed to who I am today. I feel like I've been saturated with insight but have experienced little change as a result." She was right: We spend too much time looking in the rearview mirror of life.

Learning from the Past
Any driving instructor will tell you there are necessary and appropriate circumstances when we should look in the rearview mirror: changing lanes, pulling into traffic, checking the position of cars around us, and when we hear an emergency siren coming from behind. My personal error (aside from speeding) was glancing back too often when I was driving.

In our lives, looking to the past can increase our understanding of personal strengths and weaknesses. What do I do well? What appears to bear the most fruit in my life and in the lives of those God has given me? When do I feel the most frustrated and experience a lack of peace?

Self-knowledge is different from self-centeredness. God has blessed us with the gift of reason and thoughtfulness: it is good to ponder our pasts in order to more consciously and deliberately act in the present, and make good and right judgments for the future. But my friend Kelly was on target in recognizing the limitations of seeking answers by looking only to the past.

Embracing the Present
Reviewing the past to strengthen ourselves for the present challenges of life can be helpful and a good step toward the freedom that allows us to live fully for the Lord. But along with such insight, we also need a consistent and determined effort to live a life of virtue. The *Catechism of the Catholic Church* defines virtue as a disposition to the good both in behaviors and in personal character (*CCC,* #1803). In essence, to live a life of virtue is simply to

become more like Jesus. Pope John Paul II refers to this call to be like Jesus as the "high standard of ordinary Christian living."

Virtue is not just random acts of good behavior. The fact that you gave fifty dollars to a soup kitchen at Christmas, while indeed a good action, it is not yet the virtue of charity. Giving financially to the poor or to the Church is not considered a virtue until it is habitual and firm and flows from the "good" of the person. This good act, if nurtured, could, however, *develop* into the virtue of charity because good acts are the seeds of virtues. They prepare the individual to repeat the act and as he or she does so, the desire for that goodness becomes habitual.

St. Maximilian Kolbe, a Franciscan priest from Poland, provides an example of the virtue of charity lived at an extraordinary level. During World War II he was openly critical of the Nazis. They arrested him and sent him to the concentration camp at Auschwitz where he carried on a clandestine priestly ministry, secretly hearing confessions and urging the prisoners to forgive their captors. "Hatred is not creative," he often said. Though treated as poorly as everyone else, he lived out his faith in this hell.

One day a fellow prisoner escaped and in retaliation the Nazis randomly picked ten men to die in an underground starvation cell. One of the men was married and when he cried out in despair for his family, Fr. Kolbe, who had not been chosen, stepped up to the guards and offered himself in place of the husband and father. Two weeks later he died, having helped the other victims endure their fate with courage. Fr. Kolbe's ability to step forward and imitate the sacrificial love of Jesus was the fruit of many, many good acts that formed his character and brought him to an exceptionally high standard of Christian living. At the crucial moment, he chose love.

It takes practice—often many years of practice—before good works become the habit that is virtue. Each tiny act of our day is a choice between right and wrong, virtue and vice. By consistently choosing to do good, we build a virtuous character that can withstand larger difficulties.

Putting Our House in Order

A few years ago, the letters WWJD—standing for the slogan "What Would Jesus Do?"—appeared on books, bracelets, hats, shirts and posters. Teens especially found this question helpful as they challenged each other to make good choices and to live righteously. The implication is clear: we need to become like Jesus in our thoughts and behaviors in order to make the right choices and live a good and holy life. In short, we need to live a life of virtue so that our thoughts and actions conform to the thoughts and actions of Jesus. This is the key to holiness.

What a mighty battle we fight against pride, self-will, lust, anger, greed, and envy. As if our own sinfulness weren't enough, our enemy Satan is there to stir up any trouble he can. We need to be constantly vigilant, keeping in mind the words of Jesus regarding the behavior of an evil spirit after it leaves a person. It wanders around looking for a resting place but finding none, it says,

> "I will return to my house from which I came." When it comes, it finds it empty, swept, and put in order. Then it goes and brings along seven other spirits more evil than itself, and they enter and live there; and the last state of that person is worse than the first.
>
> —Matthew 12:44-45

As we deal with sin in our lives, we become like the house swept clean and put in order. If we are to keep evil from regaining a foothold, it is imperative that we seek the Holy Spirit's help and consciously work at replacing sin with its opposite, virtue. Wayne, for example, knows that he is impatient. He finds waiting in a line intolerable; *hurry* is his only speed. When others fail to do things fast enough, he silently labels them "jerks" or stupid. One day in confession, the priest suggested a novel penance. As a way of confronting and dealing with his impatience, Wayne was to drive the speed limit all week and also pray for other drivers on the road. This was the most difficult penance Wayne ever had but he took it to heart. He wanted not only to "sweep the room clean" by repenting of his impatience but also to keep it clean by taking clear steps to overcome that impatience.

Without this sort of consistent movement toward virtue the soul remains in significant jeopardy. And we must be honest with ourselves as we examine our motives, thoughts and behaviors. We will successfully live the Christian life to the degree that we are willing to assess ourselves accurately, asking the Holy Spirit to reveal those imperfections hidden in the shadows of consciousness.

Theological Virtues

Faith, hope and love are known as the theological virtues. All other virtues—such as prudence and temperance—and all good habits are rooted in these three. The *Catechism* tells us that faith, hope and love are the basis for our moral activity and they enable us to take part in the divine nature (*CCC*, #1812). These virtues are infused, making us capable of acting as children (*CCC*, #1813). Infused is another way of saying that we did nothing to earn them, they are freely given in love by God. They are essential spiritual equipment for our journey to heaven, as necessary for our souls as air and food are for our bodies.

When we consider these three gifts, we see how closely connected sin is to virtue. So many of our unredeemed behaviors are rooted in the failure to exercise faith, hope or love. Does our critical and judgmental thinking about others stem from the failure to be charitable? Does our jealousy of others' success stem from a failure of faith in Jesus and his plan for our lives? Memorizing Scripture passages to stir faith, hope and love can be an effective antidote to these sins.

Faith. The letter to the Hebrews says that "faith is the assurance of things hoped for, the conviction of things not seen. Indeed, by faith our ancestors received approval" (Heb 11:1-2). Faith provides us with the grace to believe in God, his Son Jesus, the Holy

Spirit, Scripture and the teachings of the church. We proclaim our faith in the Apostles' Creed as we say that we "believe in God, the Father almighty, creator of heaven and earth, and in Jesus Christ, his only Son, Our Lord, who was conceived by the Holy Spirit . . .".

What faith is *not* is a commodity that you can somehow get or secure. It is not a feeling but may be mistaken for one. It is not necessary for some, but not for others. It is not an organization or a building. Faith is a gift that we can ask for and use, proclaiming it and leaning on it. I know a family beset with financial, physical and psychological struggles. Over and over and over they have withstood hurricane force winds of misfortune. They have done everything in their power to prevent or learn from these misfortunes and could, like Job, be excused if they chose to complain, whine, become bitter and resentful, blame God, and give up their faith. Instead, even though it is sometimes extremely difficult, they look to Jesus as the only Savior and Lord.

Once when Teresa of Avila was on a journey, she was caught in heavy rain and endured other woes. She complained to the Lord who replied that this is how he treats all his friends. "No wonder you don't have many," she said. There are times when we can all identify with Teresa's remark. But we must encourage each other in the truth that God loves and sustains us. When we do so, we live the Apostles Creed.

Hope. Hope fills us with a longing for heaven and gives us spiritual energy to fight temptation, resist sin and grow in holiness. It is "the theological virtue by which we desire the kingdom of heaven and eternal life as our happiness, placing our trust in Christ's promises and relying not on our own strength, but on the help of the grace of the Holy Spirit" (*CCC,* #1817).

The virtue of hope is not wishful thinking; it helps us to set our eyes on Jesus and his truth. Paul teaches us about hope in his Letter to the Romans:

> We know that the whole creation has been groaning in labor pains until now; and not only the creation, but we ourselves, who have the first fruits of the Spirit, groan inwardly while we wait for adoption, the redemption of our bodies. For in hope we were saved. Now hope that is seen is not hope. For who hopes for what is seen? But if we hope for what we do not see, we wait for it with patience.
>
> —ROMANS 8:22-25

These verses link hope with patience. We hope for what we do not yet see and patience is required until we possess that for which we hope. This is the virtue that enables us to move forward, to persevere against all odds, trusting that God's promises will be fulfilled.

Love. Paul identifies love, or charity, as the greatest of the infused virtues.

> If I speak in the tongues of mortals and of angels, but do not have love, I am a noisy gong or a clanging cymbal. And if I have prophetic powers, and understand all mysteries and all knowledge, and if I have all faith, so as to remove mountains, but do not have love, I am nothing. If I give all my possessions, and if I hand over my body so that I may boast, but do not have love, I gain nothing....And now faith, hope, and love abide, these three; and the greatest of these is love.
>
> —1 CORINTHIANS 13:1-3, 13

Of course, we are not speaking of romantic love when we speak of the virtue of charity. The *Catechism* (*CCC,* #1823) points out that charity is actually the new commandment that Jesus gave humanity: "This is my commandment, that you love one another as I have loved you" (Jn 15:12). This is the virtue that allows us to die to ourselves in service of others, in small matters and large, day in and day out. Charity inspired Maximilian Kolbe in

Auschwitz just as it inspires a home health aide to treat a patient with respect or a spouse to forgive adultery or a priest to serve his parish. This is the virtue that binds all other virtues together.

The Fruit of the Spirit

As we grow in these virtues, our lives will manifest the fruit of the Holy Spirit. Paul's Letter to the Galatians describes the works of our sinful nature: sexual immorality, impurity, debauchery, idolatry, witchcraft, hatred, strife, jealousy, fits of rage, selfish ambition, dissensions, factions, envy, drunkenness, orgies and the like. He then contrasts these with a life lived in the Holy Spirit:

> By contrast, the fruit of the Spirit is love, joy, peace, patience, kindness, generosity, faithfulness, gentleness, and self-control. There is no law against such things. And those who belong to Christ Jesus have crucified the flesh with its passions and desires. If we live by the Spirit, let us also be guided by the Spirit.
>
> —GALATIANS 5:22-25

In order for a plant to bear fruit, it must be placed in good soil, cultivated, watered, and exposed to sunlight. My husband and I lived on a small farm for ten years, an experience that helped this city girl understand some of the farming analogies used in Scripture. Up to that point, I thought fruit came from stores.

How did a nice girl from New Jersey wind up on a horse farm in Michigan? When I was pregnant with our fifth child, my husband and I looked for a house to accommodate our growing family. Our real estate agent exhausted his list of homes in the area of town we had identified but mentioned that there was a property that was different from what we had described but had the number of bedrooms we wanted—along with a horse farm, barns and pastures. My husband had fond memories of boyhood trips to his grandparents' fruit farm in northern Michigan and he eagerly set up an appointment to see the house.

We signed the papers the next day and thus began an unexpected stage of our family life. The first spring we planted a large garden: rows of corn, peas, green beans, sunflowers, tomatoes and peppers stood neatly alongside the asparagus bed and grapevines. The rich soil was a delight to see and feel. Even the older children took pride in pulling the first offensive weeds. They fought to hold the hose to water the garden and ran into the kitchen to give me daily reports on the progress of each plant. We gave guests detailed, guided tours of our famous garden.

In July we left for a two-week vacation; we returned to a jungle. Our garden was a riot of weeds that were bigger, stronger and more prolific than our little plants. The neat rows had disappeared and we couldn't even see the dirt through the tangled growth.

Each year's garden taught us new lessons. There were some things we couldn't control, like the weather, but some we could, like weeding and fertilizing. Our garden experiences eventually taught us some very important lessons regarding the spiritual life.

Gardening takes work. Spiritual growth is a wonderful combination of joy in the Holy Spirit and hard work. Pursuing virtue and becoming like Jesus yield joy as we are transformed into his image.

Gardening takes tools. Spiritually, to bear fruit, we need the daily watering and feeding of prayer and Scripture as well as advice, support and encouragement from more mature Christians. We also need more of the Holy Spirit who will strengthen and guide us if we ask.

Gardening takes vigilance. Our mistake that first summer was to think we could turn our backs on the garden for even two short weeks. Similarly in our spiritual lives we can't take a vacation from staying vigilant to sin and weaknesses. They grow like weeds and stunt our growth if we fail to pull them out.

The fruit of the Holy Spirit will be apparent in our behavior and character. As we reflect on our past and move forward in the practice of virtue, especially the virtues of faith, hope and love, our lives will reflect the character of Jesus.

Mary: Model of Virtue

One of the great graces we receive from staying in touch with our faith community is the presence of many role models. We might admire the work ethic of one acquaintance or the quiet faith of a neighbor. But our models are all likely to have some flaws. For a perfect example of virtue, we must turn to Mary.

Apart from praying the rosary, I never quite knew what to do with Mary. I understood what it meant to have a relationship with Jesus, the Father and the Holy Spirit. However, I heard many Catholics speak of how important Mary was in their lives, their love for her, the power of her intercession and the comfort she gave them as mother. But the words had little meaning for me.

Growing Up with Mary. My childhood memories of Mary center around two yearly events. When we were young, our parents established a tradition of silence between noon and three on the afternoon of Good Friday, commemorating the time Jesus hung on the cross. Usually, one or more of us kids spent that time cleaning the statue of Mary in our family's small Marian grotto. The early spring season lent itself to clearing away the leaves and debris left by a long New Jersey winter.

We honored the imposed silence and spoke in a homemade version of sign language. We became adept at inventing motions that communicated directions like, "You get rid of the leaves, I'll get a bucket of water." Reverently and meticulously we cleaned even the gross spiderwebs. I'm sure our bedrooms never achieved the order and cleanliness of that grotto. We fetched our paint pots from the basement playroom and carted them back to the grotto to repaint Mary's crumbling blue and white clothes. Then we festooned her with ribbons and early spring flowers, weaving the stems of dandelions into a miniature crown. We didn't realize that there was a difference between weeds and flowers and this freed us to admire the dandelion's early spring beauty.

I also recall the yearly May crowning of the statue of Mary, a feature of most Catholic schools in the 1950s. May is traditionally Mary's month and we said the rosary as a family as well as in school. For the girls in grammar school, much anticipation surrounded the question of who would be chosen to crown Mary. The actual ceremony centered around a procession led by the altar servers who carried the incense, the cross, and candles. Next in the procession, the chosen girl would carry the wreath of flowers and ribbons to crown Mary. We all secretly supposed that the chosen girl was the holiest and therefore worthy of the honor. I hoped that one day I would be selected.

I never was. It seemed that the chosen girl never missed a day of school, got all As on her report card, and never skinned her knee in the schoolyard. I had achieved none of those distinctions. I loved a good sore throat as an excuse to stay home from school, curled up with a book. I raced the boys at recess and came in sweaty, happy, and often with a skinned knee. And I didn't have all As. Yet I cherished the hope that somehow I might be chosen. The feeling of "not good enough" lingered. It seemed that my personality traits excluded me from being good enough for Mary.

This was my understanding of Mary as a child and I really didn't think much about her again until later in life when I rediscovered the rosary. After my conversion as a young adult I began to value the power of intercession and loved the rosary as a structured way to pray for intentions and meditate on the life of Jesus. My husband and I looked forward to drives in the car to say an uninterrupted rosary for the concerns of that day. Family devotions included each of the children leading a decade of the rosary and verbalizing their intentions (and since we have five children, the math worked out well).

Growing Closer to Mary. One day while speaking of prayer, a friend suggested that I dedicate my spiritual life to the Mother of God, and ask her to lead and guide me on my spiritual journey. I changed the subject but later that night I sat before the body of our Lord in the Eucharistic adoration chapel and pondered my apparent disconnect with Mary. My reaction wasn't negative; it was nonexistent. So I knelt before my Lord whom I did know and asked him to show me his mother whom I didn't know.

Over time the Lord answered my prayer. The connection began as I pondered my own mother's role in my life. I now understand that my mother's style of parenting was dictated by her anxiety and fear about leaving home. Home became "command central." She felt the safest there or in the yard and limited her outside activities to church on Sunday and occasional trips to the grocery store. I look back on our summer trips to the Jersey shore for a few days each year and now realize what a sacrifice my mom made in enabling those vacations to happen. She stayed in the motel most of the time and, as children, we didn't really notice or understand. This was our family, and this was our "normal." We were not abused or neglected in any way, and both our parents loved us. My dad was not only the financial provider for our family of eight but also the parent connecting us to the outside world.

This arrangement had both positive and negative consequences for me. Since my mom didn't drive, she sent me to the beauty salon in a taxi with money in an envelope and instructions for the driver to wait. She would call ahead and describe to the stylist what she wanted for me. I do remember that the women who worked there exchanged glances when I handed them my envelope. I had no idea that conducting business this way was the least bit unusual. So the quizzical looks didn't concern me.

Normal is what you know in your home and this was normal to me. At an early age I developed a competence and level of responsibility beyond most of my peers. I had to interact with storeowners, arrange transportation, and manage extracurricular activities for myself at a young age.

The Lord showed me that I was using the only model of motherhood I had and it was an unusual one. I knew love and stability and understood that my mother cared about me deeply. I did not know a mother who operated outside of home base.

Ah ha! That was the way I related—or shall I say, didn't relate—to Mary: I knew she loved me and that she took good care of Jesus when he was young but I was totally clueless regarding what she could be for me "outside in the world." Since my expectations for Mary were low, I was never disappointed. But I was beginning to find my way into a deeper relationship with Mary, Mother of all Christians.

Behold Your Mother. One of the most important recorded events in Mary's life took place at the foot of the cross.

> ...standing near the cross of Jesus were his mother, and his mother's sister, Mary the wife of Clopas, and Mary Magdalene. When Jesus saw his mother and the disciple whom he loved standing beside her, he said to his mother, "Woman, here is your son." Then he said to the disciple, "Here is your mother." And from that hour the disciple took her into his own home.
>
> —JOHN 19:25-27

This passage documents some of the last words of Jesus: imagine the pain and the effort involved for him to utter those words from the cross. Jesus not only gave John the care of his mother, he set a personal example by giving us—disciples whom he loves—his mother as well.

It was this Scripture passage that finally put Mary in my life. Mary was close to Jesus' heart as he neared death. He wasn't just ensuring her future welfare—he could have asked John at any time to take care of her. He took this personal and historic moment to draw attention to Mary and give her to *us*, his disciples. If you love Jesus, you get to love his mother as well. And amazingly, you get to have her as your mother. In that role, too, she can help heal wounds created by our biological or adoptive mothers. She is the perfect model for motherhood.

More Than a Mother. While my insight into my own mother's parenting style was fruitful, I knew that Jesus wanted Mary to be known as more than mother. As I grew in my spiritual life and read books on spiritual growth, I noticed one theme in particular: that of emptying ourselves of anything that can hinder us from being like Christ. Mary herself is a perfect example of that self-emptying, saying yes again and again. Yes to God the Father, yes to Jesus the Son, and yes to the Holy Spirit.

When we say yes to something there is the implication that we are saying no to something or someone else. So Mary's yes to the Trinity implied that she said no to other options, other roads she could have taken. She was courageous in her yes and she must have faced uncertainty as she lived that yes in her daily life. She also dealt with profound grief as she personally witnessed the physical, emotional and spiritual rejection and suffering of her only Son.

We can aspire to Mary's strength of character that allowed her to encounter everything—from angels and pregnancy by the Holy Spirit to the tortured death of her Son—with trust in God's promises. From the start, although troubled by the angel's message, she chose the righteous path even though she didn't have all the answers. She perceived herself as a servant of God and in this modeled the type of servant leadership that Jesus himself chose.

Mary is nothing less than the model of the Spirit-filled Christian. She had the mindset, the character, and the staying power that all Christians long to have. My favorite prayer to Mary as intercessor is the *Memorare,* written by St. Bernard. It describes the true state of our souls—sinful and sorrowful—implying that holiness is not the criteria for receiving mercy. Our imperfection will not be an obstacle to Mary's intercession. We can confidently go before her and beg her mercy and intervention for us and for those we hold dear in our hearts.

The Memorare

Remember, O most loving virgin Mary, that never was it known that anyone who fled to your protection, implored your help, or sought your intercession was left unaided. Inspired by this confidence, we fly unto you, O virgin of Virgins, our mother. To you we come, before you we stand, sinful and sorrowful. O Mother of the Word incarnate, despise not our petitions, but in your mercy hear and answer me.

—*St. Bernard*

For Reflection

Consider one sin that you regularly commit and reflect on its corresponding virtue.

What good acts can you do that will help you to choose the virtue you mentioned above rather than the sin? Picture when, where and with whom you commit the sin then imagine a different response. What is it?

Ask the Holy Spirit to operate more deeply in your life. (This is one thing you can never have too much of.) Close your eyes and thank the Father for the gift of Jesus and the gift of the Holy Spirit. The Father wants to give you the most precious gift of all, himself. Ask him for what you need.

Examine your values and priorities. Are they molded by your favorite television personality or are they formed in the Word of God? It helps to read Scripture so we know the mind of God. Name one value or truth or personality trait that you will explore in the Bible to see how your ideas conform to God's.

Prayer

Jesus, you know my sin, my temperament, my life. I sincerely desire to replace my sin with good acts that will help me develop virtue with the help of your grace. I long to be holy. I long to see the face of Jesus, reflecting the Father's love to me. Give me the gift of your Holy Spirit. Thank you Jesus.

Continue this prayer in your own words.

THE SIXTH KEY

FORGIVENESS

Happy are those whose transgression is forgiven,
whose sin is covered.
Happy are those to whom the LORD imputes no iniquity,
and in whose spirit there is no deceit.

While I kept silence, my body wasted away
through my groaning all day long.
For day and night your hand was heavy upon me;
my strength was dried up as by the heat of summer.

Then I acknowledged my sin to you,
and I did not hide my iniquity;
I said, "I will confess my transgressions to the LORD,"
and you forgave the guilt of my sin.

—PSALM 32:1-5

For many years my husband and I worked with students at a large public university, bringing them to Christ. To illustrate what Jesus' redemptive death on the cross meant for them personally, we briefly told them the story of salvation history ending, somewhat improbably, with the Grand Canyon.

First, we reviewed the story of Adam and Eve in the Book of Genesis, recalling that the Bible tells us that God and humans originally walked together in friendship in the Garden of Eden. When the first man and woman sinned, it created a separation between God and humanity. Imagine the Grand Canyon—God on one side, humanity on the other— separated by the effects of this sin.

God demonstrated his astounding love for us and closed that chasm in the most graphic and effective way possible: he sent his Son Jesus to die for our sins and reconcile us to himself. Now imagine the Grand Canyon. Picture the cross of Christ acting as a bridge connecting the two sides, closing the chasm between God and you.

Justice and Mercy

I imagine that when humanity rejected God's gift of total love, a gasp escaped from the heavenly chorus. First Satan rebelled against God, and then man and woman—the crown of creation—did the same. How could this be? Would mankind be condemned to the fiery pit with Satan and his fallen angels?

Offended as God was, he chose to express love again, revealing his justice and mercy. Justice demanded punishment for humankind's incomprehensible rebellion against God's love and holiness, and so our idyllic existence in the Garden of Eden ended. Now humanity would sweat and labor to obtain what once was freely given, and would be cursed with pain in childbearing. Most important, we experienced the pain of separation from friendship with God.

But mercy is the twin sister of justice, not replacing justice but completing it. In mercy, God chose not to exterminate this creation. And even though we continued to sin, he continued to draw us back to himself, even making a covenant with his people through Abraham (Gn 15:18).

When one of our children was young, she'd say, repeatedly and stubbornly, "I want to do it my own self." Despite being quite small, she tried to live without having people help her, just "her own self." Humanity seems to have the same attitude, even though this wanting to do things ourselves without the help of God gets us into trouble time and again. But finally, the cycle of salvation history brought to the fore the prophetic promise that God would send a Messiah, Lord and Savior, to free us from the devastation wrought by our inclination to do things "our own self."

The prophet Isaiah proclaimed the coming of a Messiah who would establish the kingdom of God on earth:

> Comfort, O comfort my people,
>> says your God.
> Speak tenderly to Jerusalem,
>> and cry to her
> that she has served her term,
>> that her penalty is paid,
> that she has received from the LORD's hand
>> double for all her sins.
>
> A voice cries out:
> "In the wilderness prepare the way of the LORD,
>> make straight in the desert a highway for
>>> our God.
> Every valley shall be lifted up,
>> and every mountain and hill be made low;
> the uneven ground shall become level,
>> and the rough places a plain.
> Then the glory of the LORD shall be revealed,
>> and all people shall see it together,
>> for the mouth of the LORD has spoken
>>>>> —ISAIAH 40:1-5

Recognizing Our Need for Forgiveness

We can believe that God, in his goodness, would rescue humankind over and over and over, but Christians often struggle with the concept that *they* can be forgiven over and over and over.

Take Sam, for instance. Sam was such a successful businessman that his goal was no longer to accumulate money and possessions but to take over other businesses for the sport of it. It never occurred to him that people's lives were devastated as a by-product of his conquests.

Sam grew up in a nonreligious home and needed to earn money for his family from an early age. He was a pragmatist, doing what he needed to do to survive. As he practiced his religion of pragmatism, he accumulated wealth and possessions but the initial satisfaction of financial success faded over the years. This is when he began to buy other companies even though, as soon as he acquired the company, he lost interest. He didn't care that his acquisitions left people unemployed and without benefits.

As he aged, he developed severe heart disease and diabetes and had to have coronary bypass surgery. For the first time in his life, he was confined to a hospital. Sam rarely took vacations so he found this sedentary life unbearable. But there were Christians among the hospital staff who shared with him the wonderful story of salvation and God's love for him.

True to his business instincts, he wanted to read the "contract." They gave him a Bible and he began to read a story he had never heard before. After his discharge, he continued to read Scripture and developed a long list of questions beginning and ending with the question, "Can God forgive me?"

His daily visits to physical therapy led him past the hospital chapel and one day Sam went in and sat in a back pew. Slowly the chapel began to fill as people arrived for noon Mass. He stayed. Sam knew something extraordinary was happening but didn't know what. After Mass he talked to the priest and they set up what would become a weekly meeting.

As Sam began to see spiritual realities, he confronted his desire and need to invite Jesus into his life. Sam understood that throughout his life he had been selfish, never taking anyone else's plans into account. He lied habitually, took advantage of others, swore, got drunk, used women, and generally considered others to be disposable.

The priest told Sam that he was exactly the type of person that Jesus came to save: a sinner. And yes, this good news was true even though Sam had left a trail of destruction in his wake. Sam and the priest began to study the Letter to the Romans. When they got to chapter five, Sam felt that Paul was writing to him personally.

> For while we were still weak, at the right time Christ died for the ungodly. Indeed, rarely will anyone die for a righteous person—though perhaps for a good person someone might actually dare to die. But God proves his love for us in that while we still were sinners Christ died for us.
>
> —ROMANS 5:6-8

Could this be? Christ died for him knowing that he was a sinner? Sam began to cry and his body shook as he grasped that Jesus had forgiven him by his death on the cross.

Sam grew into a beautiful, humble soul. His favorite saint was Paul, who had violently opposed the Lord and persecuted the early Christians before his conversion. Sam felt that his heart disease and diabetes were the means Jesus used to get his attention and deliver him from pride and arrogance. He thanked God daily for this second chance at life—eternal life.

Understanding God's Capacity to Forgive

Like Sam, many of us wonder if Jesus could ever forgive us. We may have one or a combination of the following misconceptions about the forgiveness of God:

1.) We might have a poor self-image, spiritually, that allows us to see ourselves as the black sheep of the family of God, unworthy of the forgiveness that God offers others.

2.) We might have high standards of holiness that neither we nor anyone can achieve. These high standards prevent us from receiving the love and forgiveness of God since we perceive ourselves as constantly falling short.

3.) We commit some sins so repetitively and habitually that we begin to see ourselves as outside of God's mercy. We are sick of confessing them and think that God is sick of them, and us, too.

4.) We have committed such serious sin we have no hope of receiving forgiveness from God.

The parable of the prodigal son in the Gospel of Luke should lay all these concerns to rest, demonstrating, as it does, the riches of God's love and mercy.

The parable of the prodigal lost son begins with the younger of two brothers demanding that his father give him his inheritance early in order to finance his travel and carousing. He squanders the money, famine falls, and he hires himself to a pig farmer, longing to eat even the scraps the pigs eat. It occurs to him that his father's hired hands live more comfortably than he so he decides to throw himself on his father's mercy and work as his hired hand.

> He set off and went to his father. But while he was still far off, his father saw him and was filled with compassion; he ran and put his arms around him and kissed him. Then the son said to him, "Father, I have sinned against heaven and before you; I am no longer worthy to be called your son." But the father said to his slaves, "Quickly, bring out a robe—the best one—and put it on him; put a ring on his finger and sandals on his feet. And get the fatted calf and kill it, and let us eat and celebrate; for this son of mine was dead and is alive again; he was lost and is found!" And they began to celebrate.
>
> —LUKE 15:20-24

Meanwhile, the older brother heard of this and was furious. After all, he had stayed and worked with his father. He had neither asked for nor received extra money or a fatted calf to have a party with his friends. He obeyed the commandments and did not sin like his brother. He went to his father and complained of this injustice. His father answered: "Son, you are always with me, and all that is mine is yours. But we had to celebrate and rejoice, because this brother of yours was dead and has come to life; he was lost and has been found" (Lk 15:31-32).

The older brother's anger seems justified. Understanding some of the historical context of this story only makes the situation worse. For example, for the heir to ask for his inheritance prematurely is the same as saying, "I'm tired of waiting around for you to die; just give me what would be due to me after your death." And the fact that the son went to a distant land meant that he didn't care if he ever saw his father alive again.

Further, pigs were unclean according to Mosaic law; the son's job was not only humiliating, it was morally unacceptable. For any observant Jew, such a son was as good as dead.

Low Expectations, Abundant Love. Realizing that life with his father, even working as a hired hand, would be better than his current existence, the son returned. His expectations were, appropriately enough, low. He underestimated his father's love. The younger man loved in a minimal way—"Give me my money, I'm out of here." He projected onto his father that same minimalist love, probably expecting his father to say, "You insulted me; maybe, just maybe, you can be my hired hand."

But the father spied him while he was still a long way off, implying that either the father or a servant was stationed at a high point on the land keeping watch for the son, anticipating, hoping, longing for his return. And even though it was undignified for the wealthy landowning father to behave in a way that did not reflect his social status, he ran off and threw his arms around his disobedient son and kissed him. And remember, the son was ritually unclean as a result of his contact with pigs and probably hadn't stopped at the local Motel Six to shower and brush his teeth, let alone perform the rituals to render himself clean according to the law.

Receiving God's Forgiveness. Jesus used this parable to show us the Father's longing for us, his watching and waiting, his readiness to embrace us no matter how sinful and stinky we are.

Read your story into the parable. You are the youngest son who has messed up, big time. Fill in the details of your own life. Guess what? God receives you with mercy and forgiveness, not recrimination, shame and guilt.

Or perhaps you are the obedient older son who has tried to do right your whole life and feel that your virtuous choices have gone unnoticed and unrewarded. Perhaps your role in this story is as the father or mother of the two sons. Have you experienced the pain that only an errant adult child can cause a parent's heart? Part of you may want to say, "Good, you got what you asked for" or demand groveling before offering forgiveness and reconciliation. Is the Lord asking you to imitate him in generosity and mercy?

The point is that redemption and mercy have won the day. This is not cheap grace. God doesn't say, "Hey, forget about it, it's nothing!" No, he makes it clear that sin is an offense to his heart of love but that his love conquers sin. None of us is the "black sheep" of the family of God and no sin is too bad or too frequent to be exempt from the love, the mercy and the forgiveness that we have in Christ Jesus. Our job is to repent and ask for the mercy and forgiveness that is already there for us.

Forgiving Others

In the Our Father Jesus taught us an uncomfortable and unavoidable truth: God forgives us our trespasses "as we forgive those who trespass against us." This might seem an impossible standard; many of us encounter one or more of the following obstacles that prevent us from putting Jesus' model of forgiveness into action. These include the occasions when others fail to acknowledge that they have harmed us and do not ask for forgiveness; when others do not show the type of sorrow we are looking for (either they don't display enough sorrow or their sorrow is not accompanied by the 'right' emotions); when the offense seems unforgivable; when we withhold forgiveness as a form of punishment to the offender; and when lack of forgiveness over time has become part of our identity.

Of course, it is necessary to distinguish between sin, which is a cause for repentance and forgiveness, and hurt feelings. Hurt feelings have unfortunately become the cultural litmus test for sin. The following examples may seem petty but they are the types of human failings often mistaken for sin: If someone didn't invite you to an event, it is unfortunate and disappointing, but it is not a sin; if someone promised to call you and did not, that is unfortunate and disappointing, but it is not a sin; if you were told that you would receive an inheritance and did not, that is indeed unfortunate and disappointing, but, again, it is not a sin. Might these events be hurtful and reflect thoughtlessness? Yes. Usually, however, they are not sins.

These people do not owe you an apology in the sight of God. It would be nice and socially satisfying for another person to understand the inadvertent pain they may have caused you through "forgetting" you. But sin is an offense against our personhood and involves such acts as lying, greed, infidelity, stealing, swearing and gossiping, among other transgressions. Hurt feelings are best taken care of by viewing the situations as disappointing and then getting on with life. This may be simpler said than done, but we cannot carry into life a suitcase full of hurts that we've accumulated over the years. It bogs us down and leaves little space for the things of God.

If someone does sin against you, it is certainly right for them to come to you, acknowledge their offense, and beg your forgiveness. Even then, you might find it very difficult to say, "I forgive you." Also, sin often leaves negative or destructive marks in our lives from which we may never totally recover. So forgiveness not only addresses the sinful action or event, it also helps address the ongoing consequences that sin has in your life. Unfortunately, some people never repent of their sins against another. In these cases, the victim has to live with the fact that the perpetrator may never acknowledge or even care about their pain.

Taking the Initiative

Amy is a good example of this challenge to forgive. When she was nine, her older brother's friend introduced her to pornography and bribed her to imitate what she saw in these movies. Acting out these sexual scenes was traumatic, to say the least. She would hide to try to avoid these encounters and attempted to tell her mom what was going on. Either Mom didn't understand or couldn't comprehend the brutal reality and told her that sometimes kids play doctor. Eventually, the boy moved and Amy never had to see him again.

The short-term consequences were that Amy became fearful and shy, clinging to her parents or teachers, and had nightmares and episodes of bedwetting. The long-term consequences manifested themselves in Amy's trouble developing normal relationships with men: when she married, she and her husband had serious problems with emotional and sexual intimacy.

Amy carried into her adult life the burden of being sinned against by this older boy along with all its consequences. She wondered if that boy ever thought about what he had done to her and if he was sorry. She wondered what she would do if he ever called or wrote to her asking forgiveness. Her Christian counselor suggested that part of her recovery from the sexual abuse was forgiving her offender.

Amy's bitterness and anger toward her offender was entrenched. "If only . . ." she often said. "If only he hadn't done this…" "If only I didn't have to deal with this…" So what does the offended person do? We join Jesus on the cross and forgive those who have offended us. Superhuman? Yes. Impossible? No. Jesus looked down from the cross and asked his Father to forgive those who were torturing and killing him. "Father, forgive them; for they do not know what they are doing" (Lk 23:34). They never asked his forgiveness; he took the initiative.

Some Effects of Forgiveness

I believe that forgiving others opens spiritual doors of grace to them. In forgiveness, we demonstrate God's mercy and love even if we can only speak through clenched teeth. It gives the offender an opportunity to receive God's grace, to repent, and to become a better man or woman. What does forgiving another do for us? It banishes spiritual, emotional and physical malaise and opens the door to holiness and happiness.

Bitterness, resentment, anger and unforgiveness—as understandable as these emotions are in response to serious sin, they grow like cancer in the spirit. Were you sinned against? Yes. Will you do what it takes to prevent the sin from spreading its malignancy within you?

Timing is important. An impulsive, hurried, perhaps superficial forgiveness will only mask the wound. Ask the Lord to prepare you to forgive your offender; he is faithful and will do it. Read books about forgiveness, including Scripture. Sometimes it can help to work in small increments. Take one part of the offense and work on forgiving just that one part. Take a break then take another part of the offense and work on forgiving that. It can also help to write a letter to your offender—most likely one you never send but that serves its purpose in offering forgiveness and helping you to state your pain.

Healing and forgiveness are linked. As we summon the courage to approach forgiveness in the spirit of God's mercy, we will find ourselves enjoying new levels of personal freedom. We will also find ourselves able to extend healing to others through the gift of forgiveness.

For Reflection

Which of the people in the parable of the prodigal son can you best relate to? How does this reflect your relationship with God?

Is there any sin, past or present, that you need to examine before the Lord? Walk through the scenario of the prodigal son and the forgiving father with this particular sin in mind.

The ability to forgive ourselves is another facet of forgiveness. Sometimes Christians can repent to God and believe that he has forgiven them but become stuck spiritually, unable to forgive themselves.

Reflect on your life to see if lack of self-forgiveness is an obstacle to your growth. Then, in the spirit of the parable of the lost son, ask the Father to embrace you and forgive you. Forgive yourself.

Prayer

> *Have mercy on me, O God,*
> *according to your steadfast love;*
> *according to your abundant mercy*
> *blot out my transgressions.*
> *Wash me thoroughly from my iniquity,*
> *and cleanse me from my sin.*
>
> . . .
>
> *Purge me with hyssop, and I shall be clean;*
> *wash me, and I shall be whiter than snow.*
> *Let me hear joy and gladness;*
> *let the bones that you have crushed rejoice.*
> *Hide your face from my sins*
> *and blot out all my iniquities.*
> *Create in me a clean heart, O God,*
> *and put a new and right spirit within me.*
>
> —PSALM 51:1-2, 7-10

Continue this prayer in your own words.

JOURNEY'S END

Then I saw a new heaven and a new earth; for the first heaven and the first earth had passed away, and the sea was no more. And I saw the holy city, the new Jerusalem, coming down out of heaven from God, prepared as a bride adorned for her husband. And I heard a loud voice from the throne saying, "See, the home of God is among mortals. / He will dwell with them; / they will be his peoples, / and God himself will be with them; / he will wipe every tear from their eyes. / Death will be no more; / mourning and crying and pains will be no more, / for the first things have passed away" And the one who was seated on the throne said, "See, I am making all things new." Also he said, "Write this, for these words are trustworthy and true." Then he said to me, "It is done! I am the Alpha and the Omega, the beginning and the end. To the thirsty I will give water as a gift from the spring of the water of life. Those who conquer will inherit these things, and I will be their God and they will be my children.

—REVELATION 21:1-7

If you are old enough to be reading this book, you have already experienced trials and troubles in life. Sometimes the trials are small, sometimes they're big, but no one escapes hardship in this world. It all goes back to the Garden of Eden: humanity couldn't last even one generation before ruining paradise.

Trials and Troubles

There are five principles that I have found helpful when discussing suffering with friends and clients. These can guide our thinking so that we are able to cope with the pain life brings our way, and respond spiritually in a way that is pleasing to God.

Principle 1: Don't be surprised when trials and troubles occur. All the trials and troubles of life stem from the entrance of sin into the world. Not only have our souls been scarred, but everything in creation has been tainted as well. When we turned from God and rejected paradise, that fall from grace had direct consequences: every woman who has borne a child understands vividly the pain of childbirth; all men and women understand the stress of financial demands as we labor for food and housing.

It might seem reasonable to be mad at God when trials and troubles occur. After all, can't he perform miracles? Didn't he rise from the dead? It might be satisfying to vent our anger but if we're honest with ourselves, we know that storming at God and asking "why" won't get us very far.

My husband and I have been blessed with the ability to bear children but the year after Timothy, our first child, was born we suffered a miscarriage followed by two more in the next eighteen months. After our losses we experienced a profound grief and asked our doctors—and God—why these miscarriages had happened.

A year or so later Jennifer, our second child, was born. After the loss of three babies, life took on new levels of preciousness. We were beaming. Then, during the next two years, we lost another baby to a miscarriage. I was psychologically, spiritually and hormonally exhausted. Well-meaning doctors advised us to go on birth control, "since we had done the best we could." Then our third child, Thomas, was born. Those early months of his pregnancy were very difficult; we prayed mightily to our Lord to allow us to have this child and were so grateful when he did.

When my husband and I were engaged, we both agreed that we wanted to adopt a child regardless of our fertility status. There was a lull of a few years after Tom was born and we asked the Lord to bless us with a child who had no parents to raise her in the Lord and in a loving family. After much prayer and effort, God answered this prayer by giving us Catherine who joined our family via airplane rather than the usual means.

Many adoptions are followed by pregnancy and we were no exception. Rebecca, our youngest child, was born a year or so after Cathy arrived. We enjoyed three years of normal family life on our horse farm in Michigan. Then on a rainy fall morning we received word that Tim, our oldest son, had drowned in a fishing accident. It was October 4, his sixteenth birthday, as well as the feast of St. Francis.

After Tim's death our life sometimes felt like Job's but with him we could say:

> I know that my Redeemer lives,
>   And that in the end he will stand upon the earth.
> And after my skin has been destroyed,
>   yet in my flesh I will see God;
> I myself will see him
>   with my own eyes—I, and not another.
> How my heart yearns within me!
>
> —JOB 19:25-27 (NIV)

Years have passed and in some ways we are all still recovering from Tim's death. Fortunately for Tim and the rest of us, he was in the state of grace when he died.

For me, asking "why" usually doesn't bring relief of any sort. Most of the time we don't understand current suffering until years later, in hindsight. At the time the pain occurs, we have no answers, just the misery set in motion a long time ago. A better question to ask is, "What now?" I've found that question more helpful in handling life's stresses and worries. For my husband and me, the answer to "What now?" is to trust in God's love for us and for our children and to rely on him daily.

We have five children in heaven and four here on earth. And the family knows who has the better deal. But Tim's death has changed us all. For him the "why" was eternal life. For each of the family members left here on earth, the why is still unfolding in different ways. The gifts of life and of each other mean so much to us. My husband and I have learned to say, as Job said, "The LORD gave, and the LORD has taken away; blessed be the name of the LORD" (Jb 1:21).

Principle 2: Examine the trials and troubles to see if they can be fixed by applying common sense.
This will sound obvious but sometimes we overlook the obvious. If you are over-scheduled, tired and crabby, deal with the problem by prioritizing your "to do" list and eliminating extra activities, even if they are good. If you are in debt and struggling financially, there are only two ways to solve the problem: earn more money or spend less. These conditions are within your control even if both are unpleasant. Whatever the situation, pray and ask God to give you the wisdom and self-control to correct it.

Generally, suffering falls into two categories: avoidable and unavoidable. Sometimes our trials and troubles are of our own making but we prefer not to look at our contribution to the problems. Sometimes our suffering is unavoidable, the result of sin and death in the world. God can give us the wisdom to deal with both.

Avoidable Suffering. Free will plays a pivotal role in avoidable suffering. We have all made decisions in our lives that we are not proud of but we have the option of learning from our sins, mistakes, habits and addictions. The challenge when we have been "young and stupid" is to not be "old and stupid." No one is pre-destined to act in foolish, sinful ways. We have free will. Although free will is what got the human race into its current condition, free will is also the means by which we can overcome the weaknesses and temptations we all experience.

One young man, Jeff, came to me for counseling for one problem but finally brought up another: he struggled with internet pornography. Embarrassed yet relieved to have finally told someone, he reported that what began as an occasional peek is taking over his life. He stays up most of the night, going from one Web site to another, sleeping late, missing class, and putting all these hours spent at pornographic Web sites on his credit card. He wept. He now also struggles with images of distorted sexuality at unwanted times: Jeff finds it difficult to think of or look at women in a normal manner.

It is a fact that pornography is not only sinful, it is often addictive. For Jeff, what started as a moment of weakness in the face of sexual temptation has become an addiction taking over a young life. The stimulating sexual scenes chemically affect the brain's pleasure center and the brain begins to crave more and greater stimulation to achieve pleasure. In some ways this stimulation works on the brain in a manner similar to that of drug, alcohol, gambling and other addictions: the pleasure center of the brain demands increasing amounts of the addictive substance to achieve the original high.

Free will also plays a powerful role in facing and recovering from sinful and addictive behavior. Jeff has a long tough fight ahead but with the grace of God and support from others he does not have to remain a victim of addiction. There are good Twelve Step programs for all types of addictions. In these, the first step is for the addict to admit that his life has become unmanageable due to the addictive behaviors, and the second step is to admit that a Higher Power is crucial to recovery (and we know who that is!).

Unavoidable Suffering. Unavoidable suffering includes sickness, pain, death, disability, physical, emotional, financial and spiritual distress that we have not set into motion through free will. Suffering would be easier to understand if only the wicked had to endure it but the young, the innocent, the elderly, the poor and the rest of us in between all have to face it. In his letter, *On the Christian Meaning of Human Suffering*, Pope John Paul II points out that "the meaning of suffering...always remains a mystery."

A close friend of mine has a daughter with Down's syndrome, a form of mental retardation. When she and her husband said yes to life they were not prepared for a handicapped child. They asked, "Why us?" Then as the Holy Spirit worked, the Lord stirred in them a tremendous love for this little one. They named her Joy since she was a powerful blessing from God to them. Of course, unavoidable suffering accompanies a situation like this but they accepted it as part of life and the Lord met them in their need. He did not heal little Joy; he changed the hearts of her parents.

Principle 3: Ask God to come to your aid with healing and miracles.

When confronted with suffering, we should pray. Jesus spent his three years of ministry demonstrating his love for us through healings and miracles. He pours out that same love today through the Holy Spirit.

> When Jesus entered Peter's house, he saw his mother-in-law lying in bed with a fever; he touched her hand, and the fever left her, and she got up and began to serve him. That evening they brought to him many who were possessed with demons; and he cast out the spirits with a word, and cured all who were sick. This was to fulfill what had been spoken through the prophet Isaiah, "He took our infirmities and bore our diseases"
> —MATTHEW 8:14-17

One day I had an infection. The site was angry red and I had a fever, headache and chills. That night there was a healing Mass at church but the last thing I wanted to do was to get out of bed and go into the chilly night air. I reluctantly went and after the prayers for healing were over, I went back home grumpy. Nothing had happened. As I got undressed for bed, I realized that the site of the infection was no longer red and tender but normal, the same color as the surrounding skin. My headache and fever were also gone. I had been miraculously healed and didn't realize it since nothing seemed to happen when I was prayed over. Joy and praise sprang from my heart.

If you are not healed or rescued from your troubles right away, keep praying. I often call friends, especially those men and women in the religious life who have dedicated themselves to prayer, to ask them to take on my prayer burden. Together we persist in prayer before the Lord, just like the widow in the Gospel of Luke who badgered the judge to act on her behalf. The judge didn't care about this woman, Jesus said when telling the parable, and ignored her. But she kept it up and he finally gave in, convinced that otherwise she would wear him out with her persistence. Just so, Jesus concluded, God will hear and answer his chosen ones who cry out to him day and night (Lk18:1-8).

Principle 4: Join your sufferings with those of Christ.
I often tell my clients that suffering cannot be measured or weighed to see what type of suffering is worse. For one individual, a mental illness that can only be treated, not cured, has the potential to make life a living hell. But a young mom with cancer suffers intensely as well. Most people I know carry some form of suffering either emotionally, physically or spiritually.

When we have applied the first three principles to our suffering, we look to Jesus on the cross and unite our suffering with his for the salvation of the world. Suffering in and of itself has no redemptive value. But Jesus elevated all suffering by embracing it on the cross: In the Garden of Gethsemane the night before he died, he had asked his Father to let the cup of suffering pass but then added, "not my will but yours be done" (Lk 22:42). In imitation of him, Christians do the same, offering their suffering for the needs of humanity.

Principle 5: Cooperate with the spiritual and character formation that trials and troubles can bring.
Amazingly, it is during trials and troubles that most spiritual growth occurs. This is often the answer to "why," only understood in hindsight. As a teenager, I didn't want my restlessness to be met by God but my life became miserable enough that I finally looked to him. That momentary suffering of depression and existential angst was the best thing that ever happened to me.

> We also boast in our sufferings, knowing that suffering produces endurance, and endurance produces character, and character produces hope, and hope does not disappoint us, because God's love has been poured into our hearts through the Holy Spirit that has been given to us.
> —ROMANS 5:3-5

Sts. John of the Cross and Teresa of Avila have developed this concept extensively. All of life can be advantageous to our journey to heaven, they tell us. Anything that is good demonstrates the love, mercy and blessings of God and any trial or trouble will be used by him to bring us closer to him and to school us in holiness.

Most of us have a junk drawer so jammed with stuff that nothing more can be squeezed in. We can only add something by removing something already there. The problem is attachment; we are usually so attached to everything in that drawer that we don't want to give anything away.

So it is with acquiring holiness: usually some things in our life need to go in order to make room for Jesus. At first, we create a relatively small space and the Lord humbly takes up residence there. We create more space as we begin to attend to the spiritual life, repenting of sin and establishing the good habits that ensure steady progress.

These tasks are the spiritual equivalent of giving away some of the items we're attached to in that drawer. But we still find ourselves reluctant to remove some of the items that crowd God out. These then become the object of more intense spiritual pressure. As the Holy Spirit directs the light of God into the shadows and corners of our life, we will beg and bargain with God, attempting to convince him that we can actually keep these attachments and still grow in love for him. Trials and troubles are often the instruments that God uses to get our attention and to pry our fingers off the things and people that we prefer to the Lord.

Especially in the higher stages of the spiritual life, suffering seems to unerringly target, with surgical precision, the exact area that the Lord desires to possess. If Christians have invested a significant amount of finances, time and personal preoccupation in social status or physical appearance, for example, often they will surrender this area of life to Jesus only when it comes under a certain spiritual scrutiny.

St. John of the Cross uses two Spanish words when speaking of this process: *nada*—nothing—and *todo*—everything. We are to give up everything and have nothing outside of the Lord. Then we will have everything: the Lord. In the process of enduring the loss and emptiness of *nada*, we gain *todo,* God himself.

This self-emptying and filling with the Holy Spirit prepares us for a deeper prayer life and ultimately, for heaven. But there is no doubt that this stripping, while fruitful, can be hard to endure.

Trials and troubles are made not only tolerable but fruitful when spiritual significance is associated with them. Look more closely when suffering occurs and hear the Lord in the details. Is he asking you to surrender in new ways that will lead to greater spiritual maturity? Is he asking you to join your suffering to his for the redemption of the world?

Never-Ending Love

Jan, a friend of twenty-some years, is a weaver. She creates tapestries and other works of art from threads and fabric. Some time ago, when she and her husband were building their country home, they included a small but airy room adjacent to the kitchen for her beautiful wooden loom.

In response to the affectionate demands of her friends, Jan demonstrated her art for us. My childhood experience of making lopsided potholders on a red metal square loom for anyone who might take one home as an act of compassion was small preparation for comprehending the complex task of professional weaving. I was astonished at the extent of planning required before Jan even attached the first thread to the loom. First, she conceptualizes the final work, developing a detailed vision of the end product. This is extremely complicated and time-consuming. Then Jan weighs the pros and cons of every potential color combination, the various textures and materials she wants to highlight and finally, the exact measurements for the future tapestry. Throughout the creative process, Jan keeps in mind the final home or destination of that tapestry or fabric art.

As she worked, I began to see the parallel between the art of weaving and the action of God in us as he weaves his work of holiness. God's work in us involves a delicate yet complex series of loving actions: his initiative and our response, both threads overlapping, blending and creating a unique yet complete work of art. The end product was in God's mind before we ever knew that a work of holiness was underway.

As a young child, I remember being impressed when someone told me that God is so great he creates each snowflake as totally different from every other snowflake. This sent me to the dining room window with a magnifying glass from my detective set. I wanted to catch God in the act of duplicating the design of snowflakes. I never did. So it is in each human life: The saving love of God looks quite different in each of our lives, a testament to his transcendent grace and mercy.

In the early stages of the holy art that is our life, the new Christian and the Holy Spirit weave the individual's efforts with the grace of God to bring about spiritual growth. As the tapestry grows—as we mature—God intervenes and we gradually begin to respond to the subtle promptings of the Holy Spirit. We give ourselves more deeply to the Trinity of love.

Along the way, we must admit and rout out addictions, curb lust through making right choices, confront laziness, put our emotions under the lordship of Jesus and so on as we move ahead to spiritual maturity. We can do these things and more through the grace that our loving Lord generously offers in prayer, Scripture, the sacraments, community, virtue and forgiveness. These six essential keys to spiritual growth strengthen, shape and purify us until we go to meet our Lord face-to-face in heaven.

As we do our part, we must always remember that underlying all our efforts is the love and mercy of God.

My husband and I are blessed with a house that has a great backyard lined with tall pine trees. To our delight, most evenings a herd of deer wanders through the yard. One day I glanced outside and thought that someone had left a jacket or a bag on the grass. A closer look revealed a beautiful fawn lying in a tight ball, front hooves tucked under its chin. It had a brown nose and a storybook coat of differing shades of tan speckled with white spots. It was early summer and we speculated that the doe had gone grazing and left the little one in our yard for a nap.

We felt strangely honored that a wild animal would deem us so safe that she would leave her baby with us. Sure enough, the mom came back and they meandered off to the trail into the woods. Amazingly, off and on for the next few weeks, the mom dropped off her baby in our yard for an hour or so.

One day, Randy ran into the kitchen to tell me that he had left the garage door open and had discovered, upon his return, the fawn in the corner of the garage. It was curled up for its nap but its eyes were open and looking at us. We approached it and it stayed still. Finally it bounded out after I "helpfully" tried to give it water. This happened several more times. We realized that during this unusually hot June, the fawn enjoyed the shelter of our garage and its cool cement floor.

Our relationship with the Lord is similar. In some ways we are fragile and easily fatigued in our journey. He is a shelter for us, his door always open for us to stumble in. We are protected from the heat of our day as we lie safely in his arms.

As we go forward with the Lord, we are looking to the true relief of suffering and stress. We look to eternal life in heaven with the Father, the Son, and the Holy Spirit. We also look forward to eternal reunion with those whom we have loved and lost. As my husband and I tell our children, now adults: we're having a family reunion in heaven and we expect you to be there.

For Reflection

The central theme of this book is saying yes to God. Is the Lord inviting you to say yes to the "more" that is unity with Jesus, the Father and the Holy Spirit? If you can't say yes, then try saying, "Help me to say yes."

In hindsight, can you see how God used suffering to bring you closer to him?

Prayer

> *Create in me a clean heart, O God,*
> *and put a new and right spirit within me.*

—PSALM 51:10

Father, Son, Holy Spirit, I love and worship you; I believe that you are opening the doors to greater unity for me. Can I come in? Is it for me, too? Summon me, your beloved, for I long for more of you.

Continue this prayer in your own words.

FROM MY BOOKSHELF

Prayer

Bennett, Dennis and Rita. *The Holy Spirit and You.* Gainesville, Fla.: Bridge-Logos, 1998.

Brother Lawrence. *The Practice of the Presence of God.* Translated by E.M. Blaiklock. Nashville: Thomas Nelson, 1981.

Cantalamessa, Raniero. *Come, Creator Spirit.* Translated by Denis and Marlene Barrett. Collegeville, Minn.: The Liturgical Press, 2003.

Chervin de Sola, Ronda. *Prayers of the Women Mystics.* Ann Arbor, Mich.: Servant Publications, 1992.

Herbeck, Peter. *When the Spirit Comes in Power.* Ann Arbor, Mich.: Servant, 2003.

Immaculata, Sister, O.C.D. *Communion with God: The Pathways of Prayer.* Bloomingdale, Oh.: Mt. Carmel Hermitage, 1981.

_____. *Guide to the Stages of Prayer According to St. Teresa of Jesus and St. John of the Cross.* Bloomingdale, Oh.: Mt. Carmel Hermitage, 1971.

John Paul II. *On the Holy Spirit in the Life of the Church and the World.* Boston: St. Paul Books and Media, 1988.

Kreeft, Peter. *Prayer for Beginners.* San Francisco: Ignatius Press, 2000.

Mansfield, Patti. *As By a New Pentecost: The Dramatic Beginning of the Catholic Charismatic Renewal.* Metairie, La.: CCRNO, n.d.

_____. *Proclaim His Marvelous Deeds: How to Give a Personal Testimony.* Metairie, La.: CCRNO, n.d.

McDonnell, Killian and Montague, George. *Fanning the Flame: What Does Baptism in the Holy Spirit Have to Do with Christian Initiation?* Collegeville, Minn.: The Liturgical Press, 1991.

Merton, Thomas. *Contemplative Prayer.* Garden City, N.J.: Doubleday, 1971.

Rosage, David, E. *Speak, Lord, Your Servant is Listening.* Ann Arbor, Mich.: Servant Publications, 1987.

Scanlan, Fr. Michael, T.O.R., *Appointment with God.* Steubenville, Oh.: Franciscan University Press, 1987.

_____. *The Holy Spirit.* Steubenville, Oh.: Franciscan University Press, 1998.

Sri, Edward. *The New Rosary in Scripture, Biblical Insights for Praying the 20 Mysteries.* Ann Arbor, Mich.: Servant Publications, 2003.

Teresa of Avila, Saint. *The Collected Works* (Vols. I and II). Translated by Kieran Kavanaugh, O.C.D., and Otilio Rodriguez, O.C.D. Washington: ICS Publications, 1976.

The Catholic Prayer Book. Compiled by Msgr. Michael Buckley and edited by Tony Castle. Ann Arbor, Mich.: Servant Publications, 1986.

The New Life in the Spirit Seminars: Team Manual, Catholic Edition 2000. National Service Committee. Locust Grove, Va: 2000.

Tiesi, Fr. Sam, T.O.R. *Remain with Me as I Remain with You.* Steubenville, Oh.: Franciscan University Press, 1990.

Scripture and Spiritual Reading

Elizabeth of the Trinity. *The Complete Works* (Vol. 1). Translated by Sister Aletheia Kane, O.C.D. Washington: ICS Publications, 1984.

Frankl, Viktor. *Man's Search for Meaning.* Translated by Ilse Lasch. New York: Simon and Schuster, 1984.

Hahn, Scott. *Romanism in Romans.* Covina, Cal.: St. Joseph Communications, n.d.

Manhardt, Laurie Watson. *"Come and See" Catholic Bible Study for Children: The Life of Jesus.* Ann Arbor, Mich.: Image Graphics and Design, 2002.

Martin, George. *Reading Scripture as the Word of God.* Ann Arbor, Mich.: Servant Publications, 1998.

Martin, Ralph. *Called to Holiness: What It Means to Encounter the Living God.* San Francisco: Ignatius Press, 1999.

_____. *Hungry for God.* San Francisco: Ignatius Press, 2000.

Matthew, Iain. *The Impact of God.* London: Hodder and Stroughton, 1995.

Nouwen, Henri J.M. *The Return of the Prodigal Son: A Story of Homecoming.* New York: Doubleday, 1994.

Perrotta, Kevin. *Your Invitation to Scripture: An Intorduction to the Bible for Catholics.* Ann Arbor, Mich.: Servant Publications, 2003.

Ponessa, Fr. Joseph, S.S.D., and Manhardt, Laurie Watson. *Come and See Catholic Bible Study: John.* Self-published, 2002.

Saint-Jure, Fr. Jean Baptiste, S.J., and de la Colombiere, Blessed Claude, S.J. *Trustful Surrender to Divine Providence: The Secret of*

Peace and Happiness. Translated by Paul Garvin. Rockford, Ill.: Tan Books and Publishers, Inc., 1983.

Schlink, Basilea. *You Will Never Be the Same.* Minneapolis: Dimension Books, 1972.

Shields, Sr. Ann, S.G.L. *Yielding to the Power of God.* Steubenville, Oh.: Franciscan University Press, 1991.

Winzen, Damasus. *Pathways in Scripture.* Ann Arbor, Mich.: Servant. 2003.

Sacraments

Arinze, Cardinal Francis. *The Holy Eucharist, Christ's Inestimable Gift.* Huntington, Ind.: Our Sunday Visitor Press, 2001.

Bernadot, M.V. O.P. *The Eucharist and the Trinity.* Translated by Dom Francis Izard, O.S.B., and Penny Livermore. Wilmington, Del.: Michael Glazier, Inc., 1977.

De Grandis, Fr. Robert, S.S.J. *Receiving Holy Eucharist, The Sacrament of Healing.* N.p.: Praising God Catholic Association of Texas, 1996.

Hahn, Scott. *The Lamb's Supper.* New York: Doubleday, 1999.

Community

John Paul II. *The Lay Members of Christ's Faithful People.* Boston: Daughters of St. Paul, 1989.

_____. *Letter of Pope John Paul II to Women.* Boston: St. Paul Books and Media, 1995

_____. *Novo Millennio Ineunte.* Boston: St. Paul Books and Media, 2001.

_____. *The Role of the Christian Family in the Modern World.* Boston: Daughters of St. Paul, 1982.

Virtue

Bodo, Murray, O.F.M. *Through the Year with St. Francis of Assisi.* Cincinnati: St. Anthony Messenger Press, 1993.

Cantalamessa, Raniero. *Life in the Lordship of Christ.* Translated by Frances Villa. Kansas City: Sheed and Ward, 1989.

Cavnar, Cynthia. *Prayers and Meditations of Thérèse of Lisieux.* Ann Arbor, Mich.: Servant Publications, 1992.

_____. *The Saints from A to Z.* Ann Arbor, Mich.: Servant Publications, 2000.

Ciszek, Walter, S.J. *He Leadeth Me.* Garden City, N.J.: Doubleday, 1975.

Daughters of St. Paul. *Fifty-Seven Saints for Boys and Girls.* Boston: Daughters of St. Paul, 1980.

De Caussade, Jean-Pierre. *The Sacrament of the Present Moment.* Translated by Kitty Muggeridge. San Francisco: Harper, 1989.

DeMarco, Donald. *The Heart of Virtue.* San Francisco: Ignatius Press, 1996.

DeSales, Saint Francis. *Introduction to the Devout Life.* Translated and edited by John Ryan. New York: Image Books, 1989.

Dubay, Thomas, S.M. *Seeking Spiritual Direction: How to Grow the Divine Life Within.* Ann Arbor, Mich.: Servant Publications, 1993.

Ghezzi, Bert. *Voices of the Saints: A Year of Readings.* New York: Doubleday, 1991.

Groeschel, Benedict, C.F.R. and Montini, James. *Praying in the Presence of Our Lord with the Saints.* Huntington, Ind.: Our Sunday Visitor Press, 2001.

Immaculata, Sister, O.C.D.. *A Study of Conscience.* Bloomingdale, Oh.: Mt. Carmel Hermitage, 1970.

John of the Cross, Saint. *The Collected Works of St. John of the Cross.* Translated by Kieran Kavanaugh, O.C.D., and Otilio Rodriguez, O.C.D. Washington: ICS Publications, 1991.

John Paul II. *Mary: God's Yes to Man.* Introduction by Joseph Cardinal Ratzinger and Commentary by Hans Urs von Balthasar. San Francisco: Ignatius Press, 1988.

Payesko, Robert J. *The Truth about Mary: A Summary of the Trilogy.* Santa Barbara, Cal.: Queenship Publishing, 1988.

Pinckaers, Servais, O.P. *The Pursuit of Happiness—God's Way: Living the Beatitudes.* Translated by Sr. Mary Thomas Noble, O.P. New York: Alba House, 1998.

Teresa of Avila, Saint. *The Collected Works* (Vols. I and II). Translated by Kieran Kavanaugh, O.C.D., and Otilio Rodriguez O.C.D. Washington: ICS Publications, 1976.

Thérèse of Lisieux, Saint. *Story of a Soul.* Translated by John Clarke, O.C.D. Washington: ICS Publications, 1996.

Van Breemen, Peter, S.J. *As Bread that is Broken.* Denville, N.J.: Dimension Books, 1974.

Forgiveness

McAlear, Fr. Richard, O.M.I. *Forgiveness: Experiencing God's Mercy.* Self-published, 2002.

_____. *Healing.* Self-published, 1999.

Monobourquette, John. *How to Forgive: A Step-by-Step Guide.* Cincinnati: St. Anthony Messenger Press, 1999.

General Reference

Catechism of the Catholic Church. Washington: USCC, 1994.

The Catholic Encyclopedia. Edited by Robert C. Broderick. Nashville: Thomas Nelson, 1987.

Documents of Vatican II: In a New and Definitive Translation with Commentaries and Notes by Catholic, Protestant and Orthodox Authorities. Edited by Walter M. Abbott, S.J., America Press, 1966.

Schreck, Alan. *Catholic and Christian: An Explanation of Commonly Misunderstood Catholic Beliefs.* Ann Arbor, Mich.: Servant Publications, 1984.

ABOUT THE AUTHOR

Therese Cirner is a licensed clinical counselor, speaker and author. She and her husband Randall live in Florida and are the parents of five children and one grandchild. For additional information, see her Web site: www.theresecirner.com.